OLD TIME String Band Banjo Styles

By Joseph Weidlich

ISBN 978-1-57424-299-7
SAN 683-8022

Cover by James Creative Group

P.O. Box 17878 - Anaheim Hills, CA 92817

www.centerstream-usa.com

Library of Congress Photograph.

TABLE OF CONTENTS

INTRODUCTION

The focus of this book is to provide an overview of the basics of old time string band banjo styles as played in the Southern mountains of the eastern United States for "seconding" vocal songs and fiddle tunes. I am going to look at those techniques principally in the context of Golden Age string band recordings, i.e., directly from the backups of string bands on recordings issued for commercial retail sale during the 1920s and very early 1930s. Many of those bands were initially recorded by major record companies during field recording trips that they conducted in the South for inclusion in either their "race" or "hillbilly" record categories. If enough copies of a particular "side" sold then those groups would often be invited to travel to a record company's professional facilities for additional recording sessions.

Due to the poor audio balance found on many of those historic recordings it is often difficult to always follow what the banjo is doing because it is competing sonically with the fiddle, voice and guitar. One key element in trying to determine which banjo style might be being used is to attempt to identify which beat that the higher-pitched open fifth string drone note falls on: if it fell on the downbeat then the technique used might be thumb lead; conversely, if it fell on the upbeat then it might be index lead. Another variable, particularly in the clawhammer performance style, was the use of altered tunings in place of the standard C or open G tunings.

Also included here is detailed information on the influence of the classic and ragtime banjo performance styles on the string band genre, as popularized, for instance, by Charlie Poole on his recordings with his North Carolina Ramblers.

These four performance styles -- banjo style, guitar style, index lead and thumb lead -- formed the nucleus of the traditional, rural string band banjo style. It is interesting to note that even as the harder-driving, syncopated three-finger picking "Scruggs style" was growing in popularity in the late 1940s and early 1950s many "old time" banjo players, who were "rediscovered" during the folk music revival of the late 1950s/early 1960s, remained true to the their traditional "roots" performance style: many chose not to "convert" to the newer bluegrass style of playing.

Charlie Poole, center, and The North Carolina Ramblers, Posey Rorer and Roy Harvey, in the 1920's.

PART I: HISTORICAL BACKGROUND

In 1839, the year C.F. Martin moved his guitar making operation from New York City to Nazareth, Pennsylvania, an important collection of 35 fiddle tunes was published by the Baltimore publisher, George Willig, Jr., "selected and arranged for the pianoforte" by George P. Knauff. This collection of four volumes, entitled *Virginia Reels*, is particularly important as it is believed to be the only substantial extant compilation of nineteenth-century Southern fiddle tunes published prior to the Civil War.

This collection is particularly important because it seems clear that Knauff was familiar with the banjo, or at least with its basic accompaniment rhythms, because he used two stock banjo licks in two of those arrangements: *Sich a gittin up stairs* [Section B2] and *Ohio River* [Section A]. Those "licks" were the quarter note followed by two eighth notes rhythmic unit (in 2/4 time they would be written as an eighth note followed by two 16th notes), while the second was the double-thumbing technique (for additional information on the Knauff collection please see my book on the *Virginia Reels*). Thus, those two principal idiomatic banjo "movements" were in use years before the popularity of the minstrel show emerged with the sudden popularity of the Virginia Minstrels in New York City in early 1843, and the banjo, as a characteristic folk instrument, along with it.

Thus, the basic rhythmic unit of the urbanized "banjo style," associated with antebellum minstrel stage performances, was what Pete Seeger later phonetically referred to as "bum-titty" in his famous banjo method, *How to play the 5-string Banjo* (first published in 1948). The second rhythmic figure was sometimes referred to as the *double strike*, what we now often refer to as *double thumbing*. Also, the fifth string played open could be used as either an independent melodic note or as a drone note.

"BANJO" STYLE

The original manner of playing the banjo, learned directly from African-American slaves, was called the "banjo" or "stroke" style that used the index finger to <u>strike</u> <u>down</u> on the long strings of the banjo while the thumb played the open fifth string. The banjo began to become popular in urban areas because of its inclusion in the instrumentation (fiddle, bones, tambourine and banjo) used in the early minstrel shows (beginning from1843). This down-picking method of playing is today referred to as clawhammer performance style. Those idiomatic techniques remained basically unchanged except for the development of altered tunings "at the South," used to accompany modal tunes and songs, in the first decades of the 20th century (for a more detailed examination on the development of this original style of playing the banjo please see my book, *The Early Minstrel Banjo: Techniques and Repertoire*).

The original style of banjo performance is based on a number of rhythmic "movements," the basic ones being the rhythm of a quarter note-two eighth notes (I IT), the other being the double thumbing note sequence (ITIT), i.e., four eighth notes in succession with the thumb playing its notes on 2 and 4. Here is what it looks like in tablature:

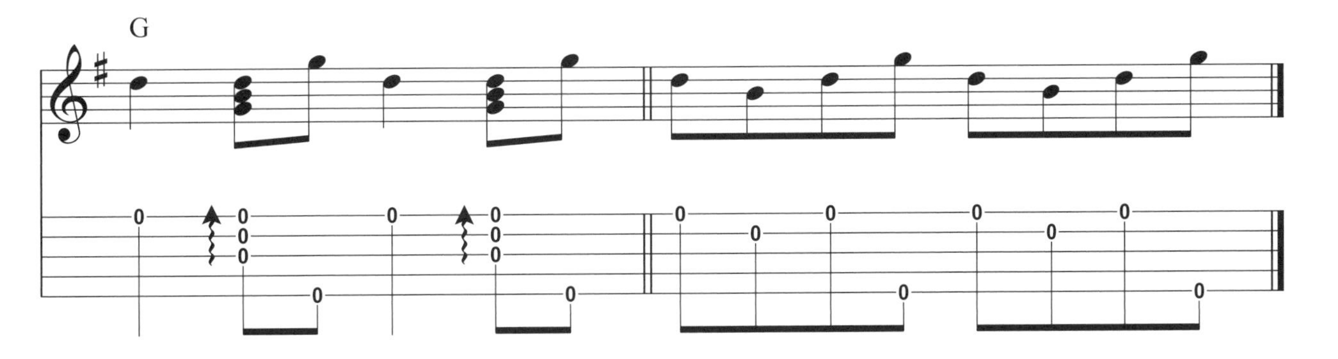

The brush stroke used in the basic strum is often replaced by just playing the first string alone, sometimes referred to as brushless strumming:

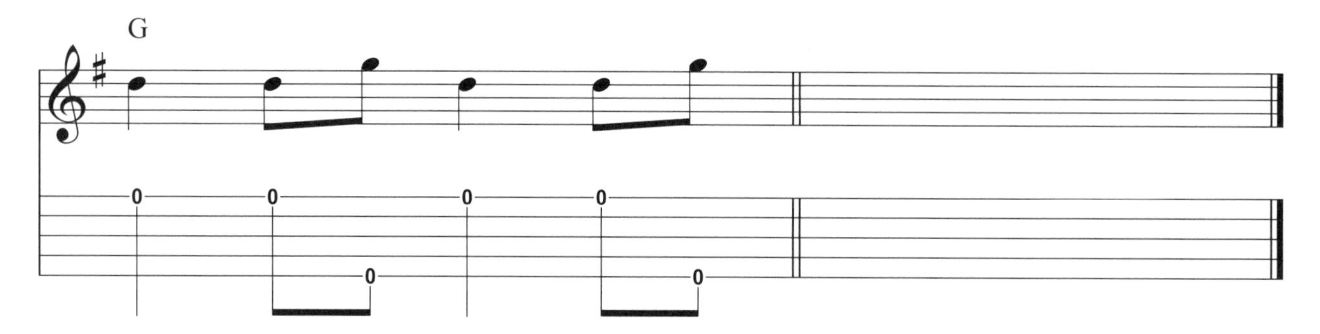

Left hand embellishments were often interpolated, i.e., hammer-ons and pull-offs (including open-string pull-offs), and some fancy triplet licks as well.

The following arrangement of *Arkansas Traveler*, as published in Frank Converse's *Banjo Instructor, Without A Master* (1865), aptly demonstrates the "banjo" style of performance. While the song was published in 2/4 time using a dotted hornpipe rhythm, I am using standard eighth notes rhythm here for purposes of visual clarity:

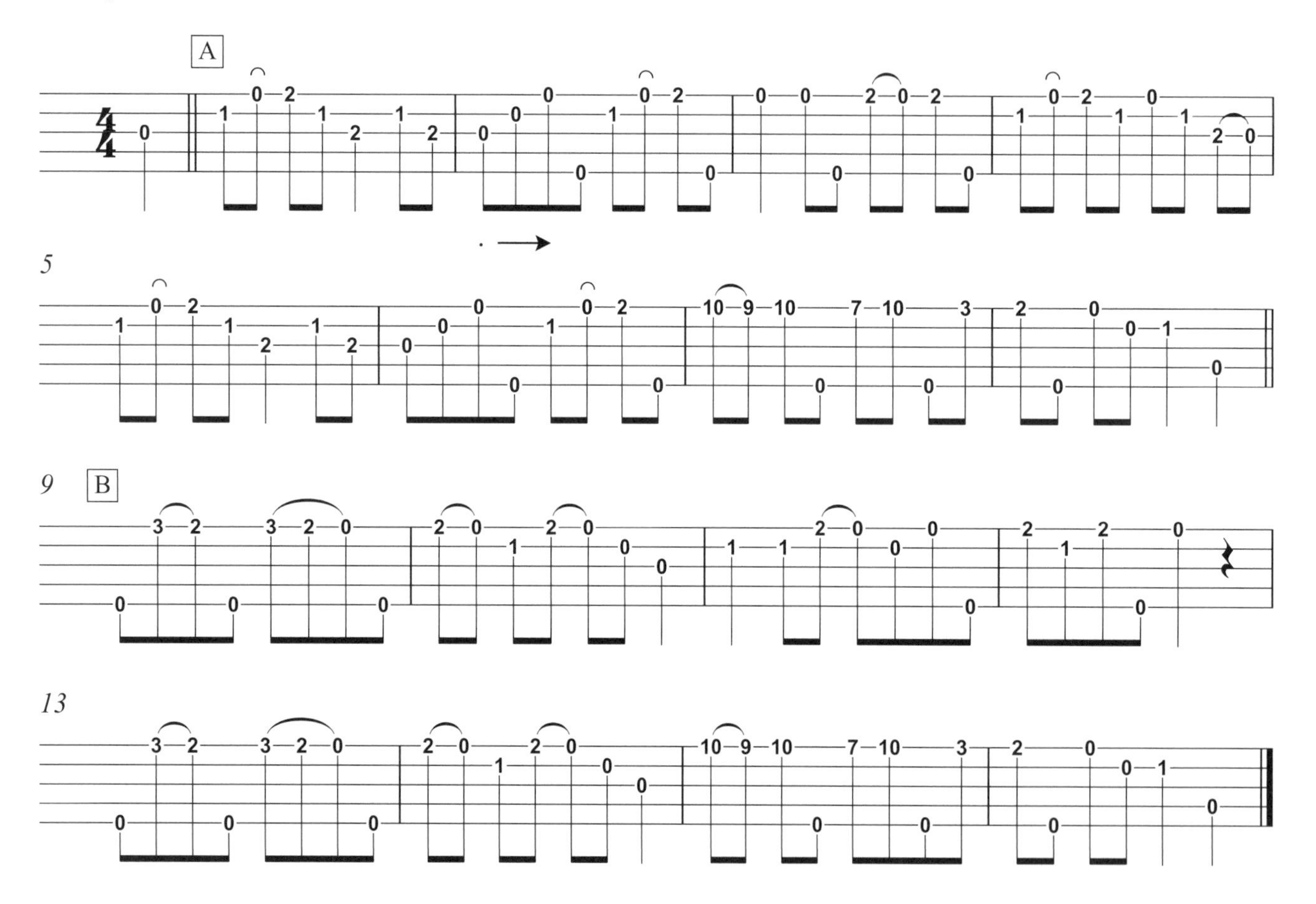

Special Left Hand Articulations. You can add left hand articulations, such as hammer-ons, pull-offs, or (later) slides, to embellish the main melodic notes. A special pull-off technique that dates to the antebellum minstrel banjo period is today called an "open string pull-off." Use of this technique was notated in those banjo methods by use of a semi-circle over a note. In the first two examples below position the second finger of your left hand on the second fret of the first string and simply pull it off, i.e., sideways, away from the edge of the fingerboard, on the upbeat, creating an open first string note <u>without</u> <u>striking</u> <u>that</u> <u>string</u> with the index finger:

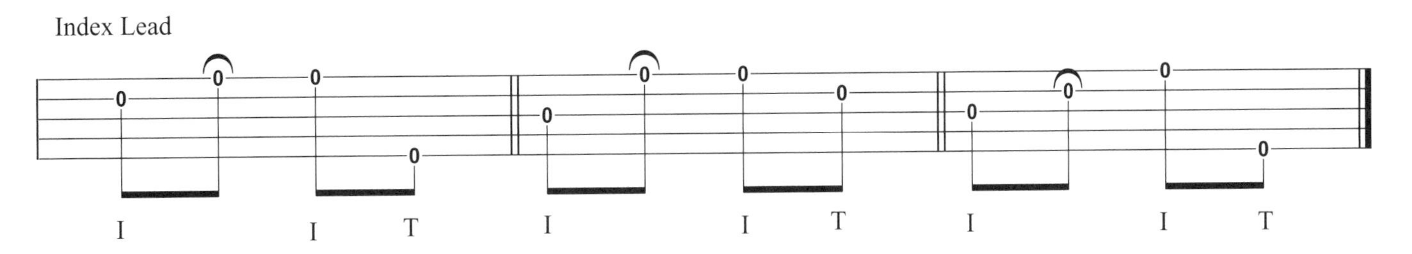

A parallel articulation evolved in that hammer-ons could be executed by simply "hammering" down on a fret without any right hand preparation, called, appropriately enough, an "open string hammer-on."

Here is a banjo tab for the song *Lynchburg Town* as found in Frank Converse's *New and Complete Method for the Banjo with or Without A Master* (published 1865). Note that in this song the open string pull-off occurs on both the first <u>and</u> second strings:

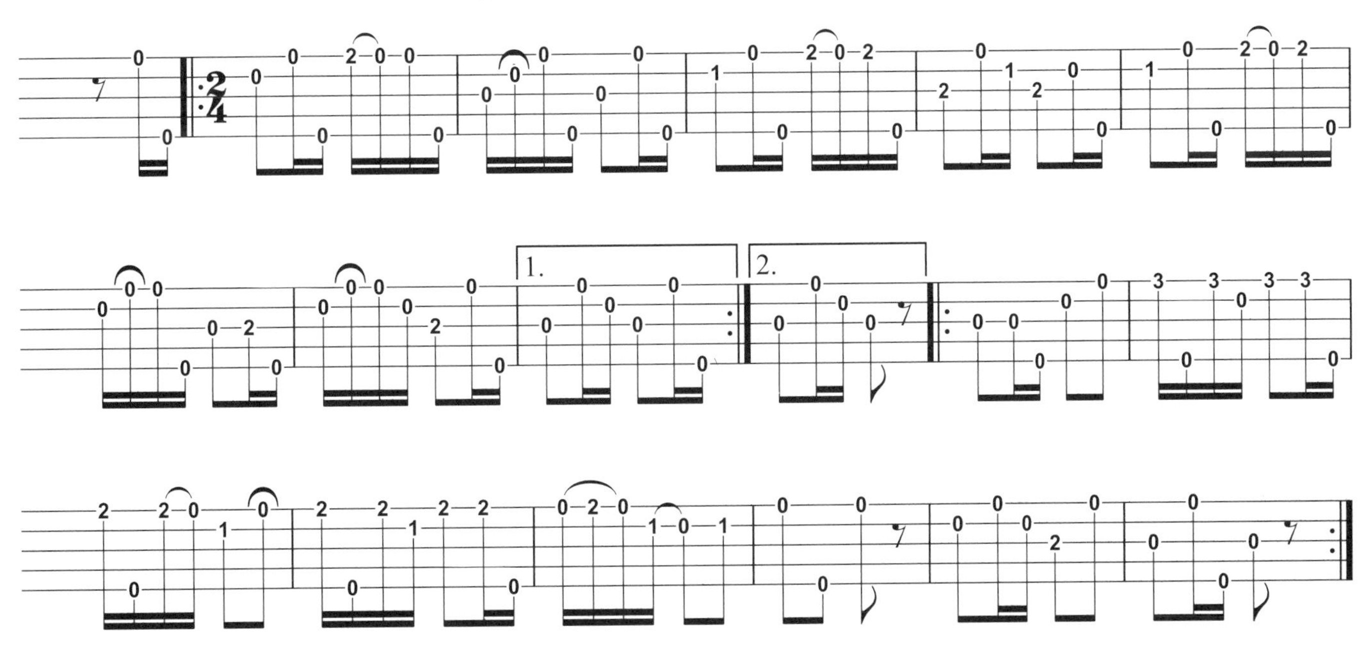

The use of the open string pull-off technique was documented in 1858 in Phil Rice's *Correct Method for the Banjo*. Also, note the use of the fifth string as a melody note (e.g., in measures 7 and 8), an early form of the "Galax lick" roll pattern (e.g., in measure 2), and the use of playing consecutive notes with the same rhythm by the index finger (a common right hand technique at that time).

"GUITAR" STYLE

By the time the first banjo methods began to be published in the late 1840s and 1850s some of them began to call attention to an alternate way to approach playing the instrument, called "guitar style". How did this development come about?

There were a number of guitar methods available in the U.S. from the 1820s on, e.g., the first American/ English edition of the popular Carcassi Method for classic guitar became available in the 1840s. The high level of interest in playing the guitar is reflected in the fact that a number of luthiers began to make guitars commercially in the United States, e.g., C.F. Martin from 1833. Due to the immense popularity of the minstrel show genre beginning in 1843 and, as the minstrel songs associated with it had been "in the air", the genteel parlor guitar finger style technique was easily transferred over to the banjo. For instance, Tom Briggs introduces the use of "guitar style" for the accompaniment to the vocal songs in his method (*Briggs Banjo Instructor* [1855]), which were modeled after typical parlor guitar accompaniment patterns.

While the original banjo style didn't disappear from the many new banjo methods published during the second half of the 19th Century there was a gradual shift in emphasis from the original style of playing the banjo, and its characteristic repertoire, to the developing parlor guitar style used to arrange, for instance, European-based songs (operatic and otherwise) and new dance forms that eventually blossomed into the intricate "classic banjo" performance style.

Let's look at some commonly used parlor guitar backup techniques as found in the *Dobson Brothers' Modern Method for the Banjo* (1871), as these examples are typical of those used later by Southern string band banjoists. The example below is a standard accompaniment pattern:

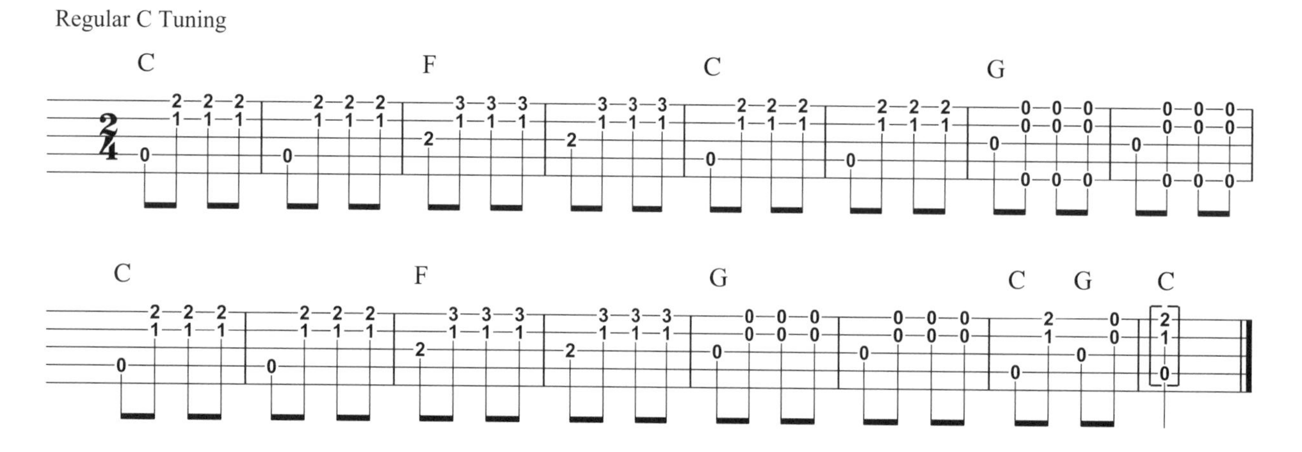

Most of the time the index and middle fingers are used to play the notes on the first two strings.

Here is a backup to the song *Don't You Wish You Could*, found on page 44 of Dobson. It utilizes arpeggiated chord outlines, including one fingering "up the neck" in the fifth position:

Regular C tuning

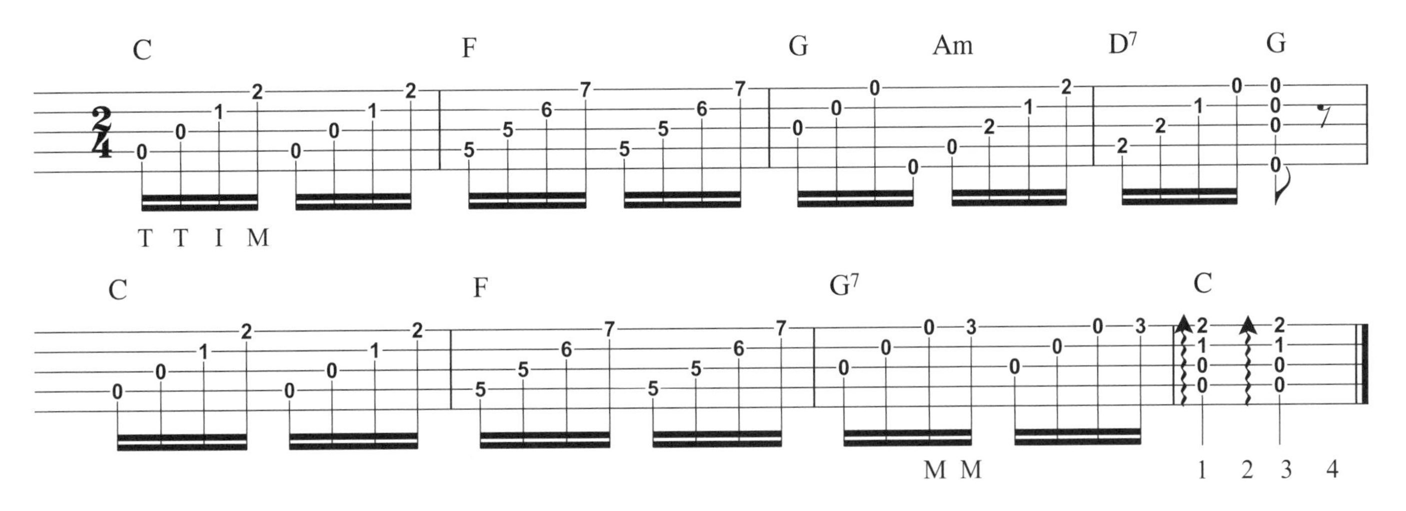

Note here that the thumb is used twice in succession to outline the arpeggios in this example (probably via a glide stroke). Normal technique of the time would have been to play notes on the fifth or fourth strings with the thumb, notes on the third string with the index finger, notes on the second string with the middle finger, and notes on the first string with the ring finger.

The backup to Exercise #3 uses four 16th notes followed by a pair of eighth notes throughout:

Regular C tuning

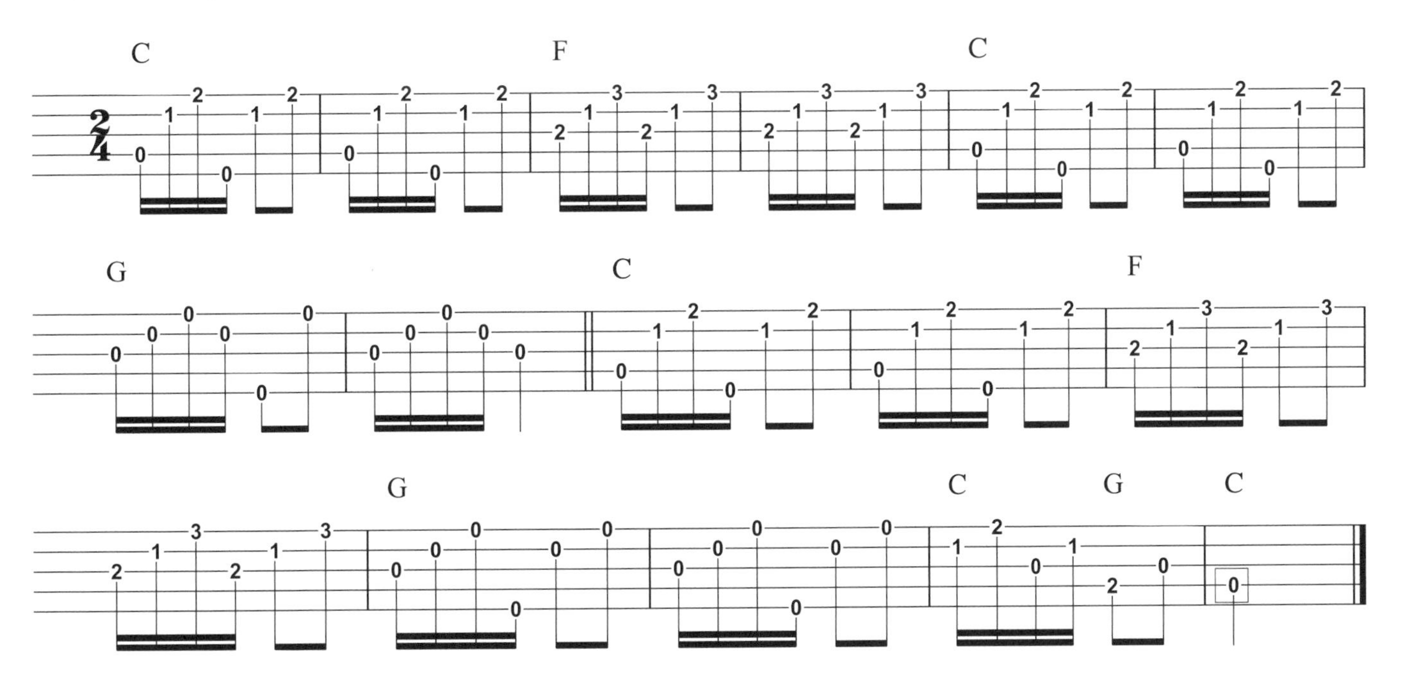

Let's expand on these ideas by presenting the backup to the song *Little Mary Polka* (found in Part II, Vocal and Instrumental Amusements, on page 39):

Regular C Tuning

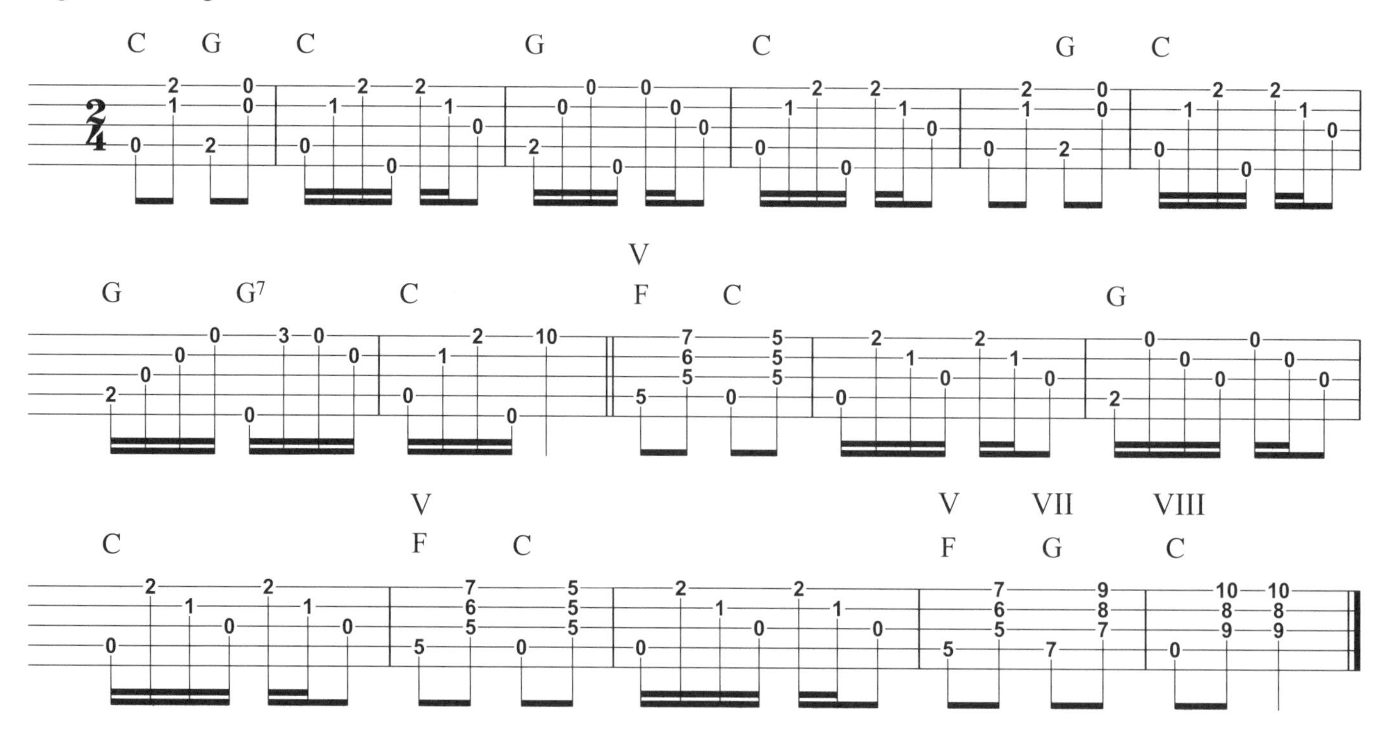

The outlines used in measures 2, 3, and 4 resemble a bluegrass banjo forward-reverse roll, while at measures 10, 11 and 12 a backwards-type roll is used. "Up the neck" block chords are used at measures 9, 13, 15 and 16.

THE CLASSIC AND RAGTIME BANJO PERFORMANCE STYLE

With the emergence and popularity of ragtime piano music in the late 19th century, and the parallel invention of a system of audio recording by Thomas Edison at about the same time, the popularity of the banjo increased to new heights by its ability to render ragtime tunes that featured the characteristic syncopation inherent in the banjo's African origins made popular via the minstrel show genre. With the growing popularity of those recordings, publishers began to supply ragtime-influenced sheet music for the banjo once it became clear that there was a demand for it. Two of the most widely recorded banjo artists of that period were Sylvester "Vess" Ossman [1868-1923] and Fred Van Eps [1878-1960]. Ossman, widely known as "The Banjo King," was one of the first to make commercial banjo recordings beginning around 1893 while Van Eps was one of the most recorded banjoists in America in the post-ragtime era (his first cylinder recordings were made ca. 1897-98 for the United States Phonograph Company in Newark, NJ, owned by Thomas Edison).

As a point of information for those interested, by 1860 the staff notation for banjo music was more or less established as being played and written in two principal keys: A (three sharps) and E (four sharps). By the turn of the century those keys would evolve to today's standard keys of C and G, respectively. However, the peculiarity of this is that while the tuning of the banjo gradually changed in pitch (eventually a minor third higher, from A to C) it was still being written in the keys of A and E (historically referred to as "A" Notation). Around 1900 this notational system began to be updated when music for the banjo began to be written at concert pitch. This new practice is reflected with the publication of a number of new banjo methods around that time, such as *The 20th Century Method for the five string Banjo* (Universal Notation) by J.E. Agnew (first published in 1901 by Agnew, with several later editions including one reprinted as late as 1941 by Volkwein Bros., Inc., in Pittsburgh, PA). That being said, it would be some years before this universal notation practice began to be commonly used in printed music for the banjo. All of the staff notations in this book are based on concert pitch, unless otherwise noted.

As I will mention elsewhere from time to time, because the classic banjo compositional style is not based on the use of right hand rolls, i.e., incorporating melodic notes within a roll pattern, some of the classic banjo patterns can, nonetheless, sound like traditional banjo rolls, particularly when classic banjoists use just the thumb, index and middle fingers.

Sam and Kirk McGee flank Arthur Smith.

To conclude this section I would like to present the first section of a musical composition entitled *The Tubaphone Rag*, which was written as a dedication for that famous banjo tone ring. This arrangement is typical of Charlie Poole's performance style:

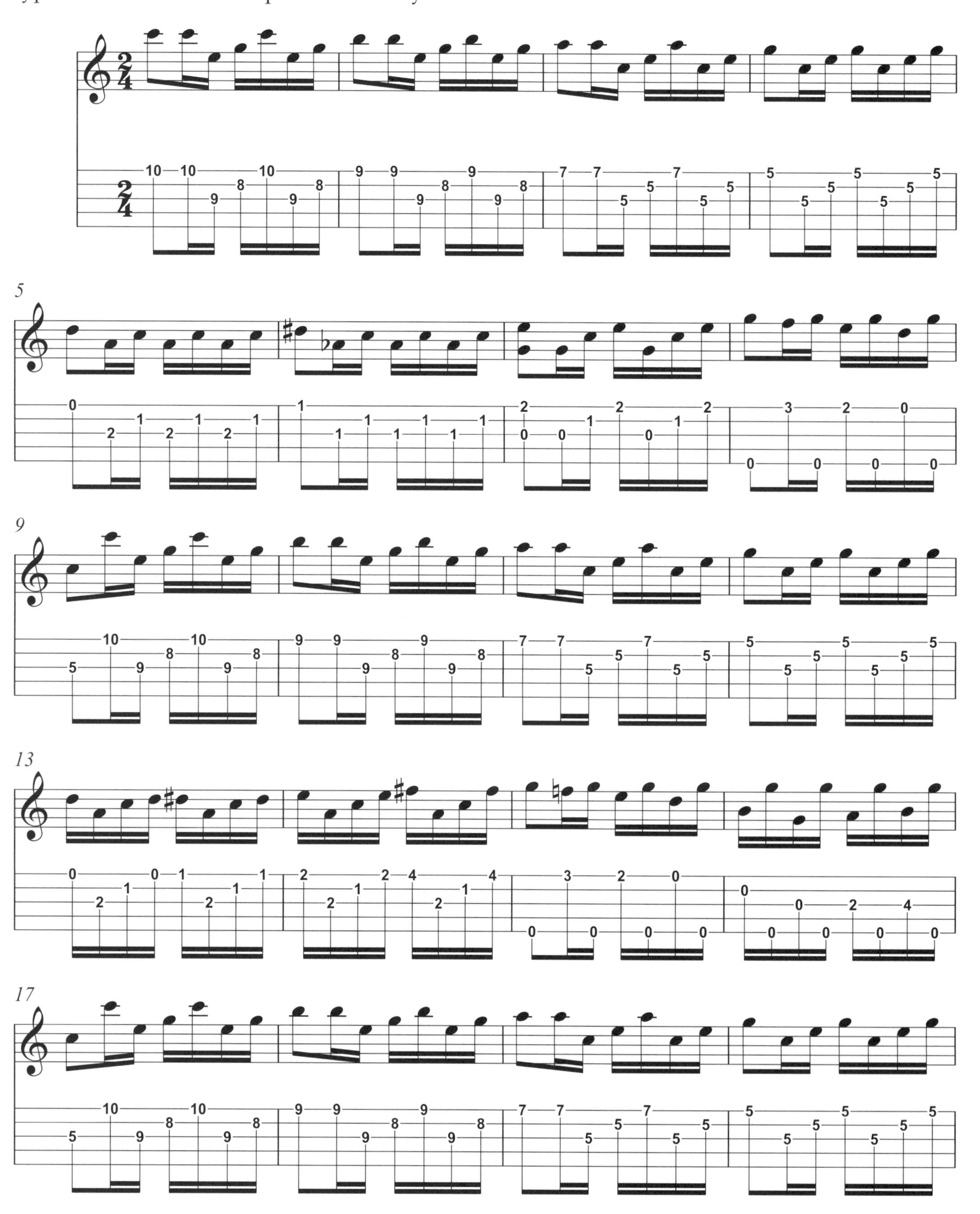

2-FINGER TECHNIQUES

INDEX-LEAD STYLE BASICS

The index-lead banjo style is the transformation of the traditional, down-picking style to an up-picking style in which the right hand index finger, instead of striking down, picks those notes "up," by adapting the parlor guitar finger picking. Thus, you can, in theory, play most any stroke style banjo arrangement by substituting the guitar style for it.

Let's begin by outlining the basic note sequences, or "movements," idiomatic to the index-lead style. The most basic movement is simply to play melody notes with the index finger on the beat (in these initial examples the "x" as the note head represents any melodic note; the dot below a stem indicates that note is to be played by the index finger):

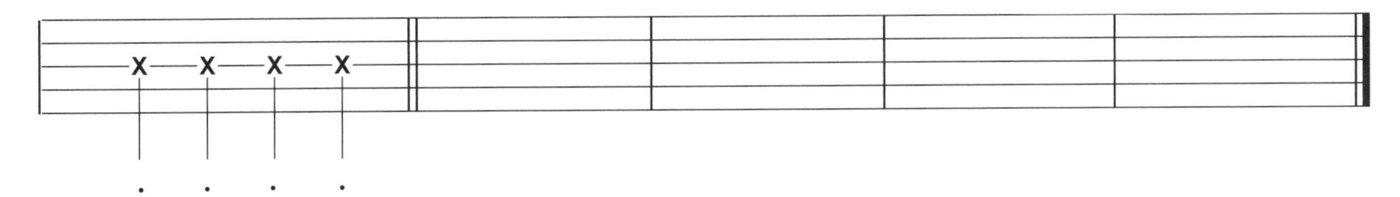

The thumb can then be used to play a drone note on the fifth string in between the beats (here notated by the smaller "x" found below the note beams):

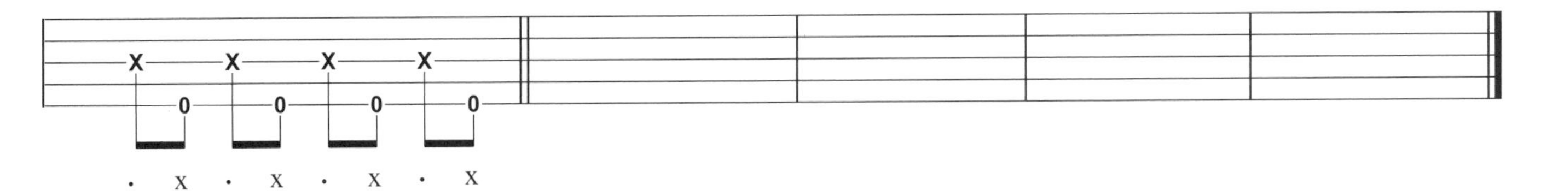

Here is how the traditional banjo rhythm of a quarter note and two eighth notes appears when written out in banjo tablature:

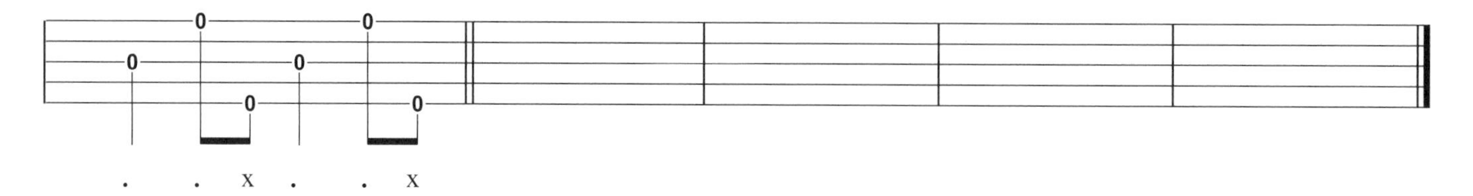

Next is the commonly used *double thumbing* technique, followed by an example of two consecutive drop thumbs (historically referred to as a *double-double*):

Double-Thumbing Technique: Double-Double Technique:

Here is an example of a moving melodic line on the first string using, primarily, the double-thumbing technique:

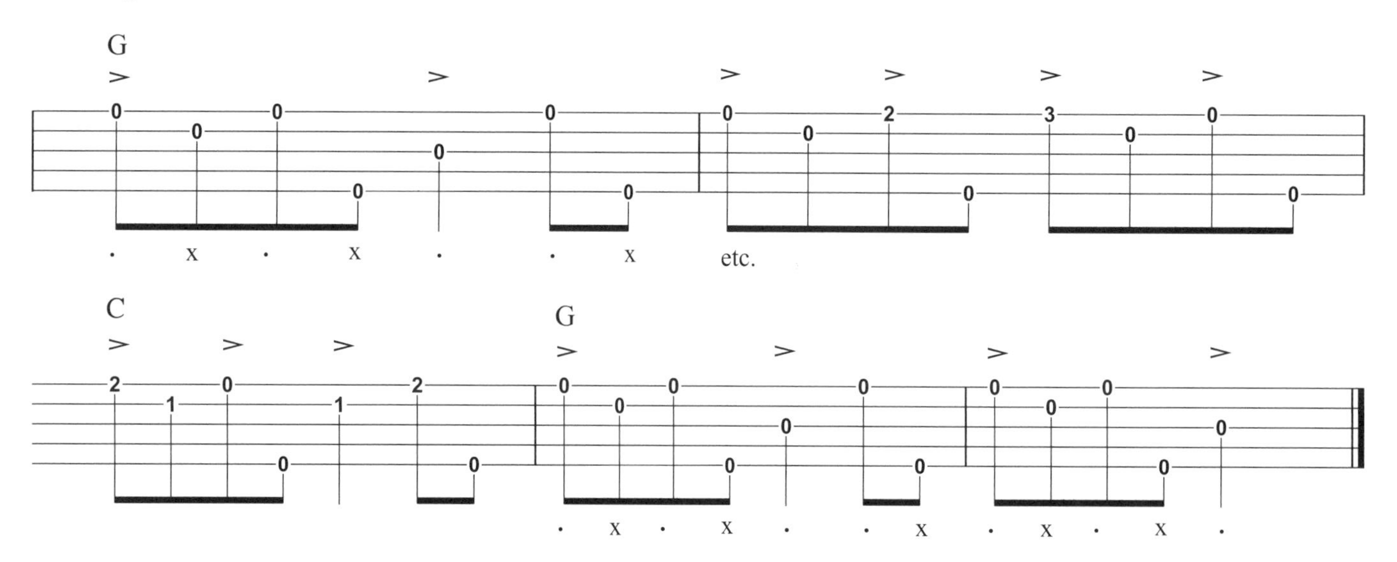

In the index-lead style the first two strings can also be struck by an upwards movement of the index finger instead of just the first string. This was an idiomatic performance practice used by North Carolina country lawyer/folklorist Bascom Lamar Lunsford. When Pete Seeger first began to play banjo in the mid-1930s he was fortunate to have had the opportunity to observe Bascom Lunsford's playing style close up, so his style had a large impact on Seeger's development of a basic strum for his own personal backup style. This became an important element of the "Seeger style" (the "-titty" part); however, while Seeger used an upward stroke on the single quarter note beat, as did Lunsford, Seeger then followed that by playing a downward brush of the right hand fingers (or just his ring finger) in his basic strum pattern (instead of an upstroke/strum, as Lunsford did), followed by playing the open fifth string with his thumb:

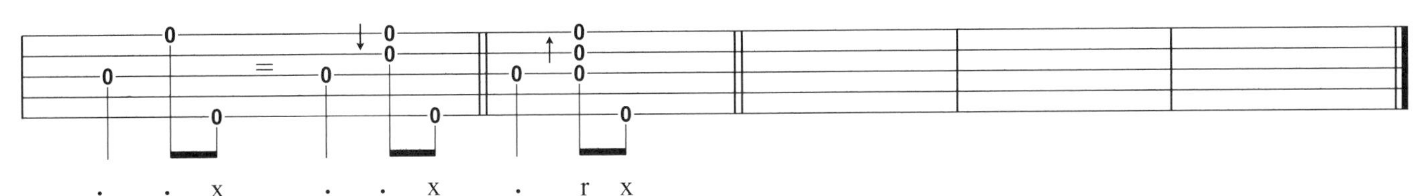

THUMB-LEAD STYLE BASICS

Thumb-lead style is the reverse of index-lead in that the thumb plays the melodic notes and the fifth string on the beat; the index finger plays the first string (secondary drone) on the off beats, thus the melodic line is usually played on the second, third and fourth strings. From a gravitational point of view, as the thumb is striking down on the downbeats, that makes for a stronger sound (as does, for the same reason, the down-picking clawhammer style).

As in index-lead, melodic notes in thumb-lead style can be played as individual notes, this time by the thumb:

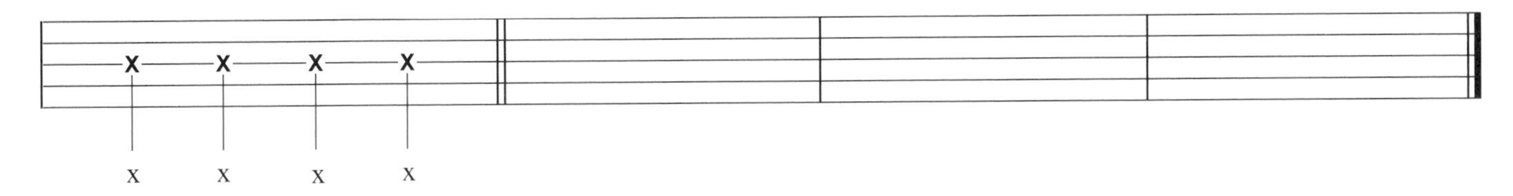

Melodic notes are often alternated with the first string drone note, which is played on the offbeat, or only on the upbeats of beats 2 and 4, which reinforces the traditional basic banjo rhythm:

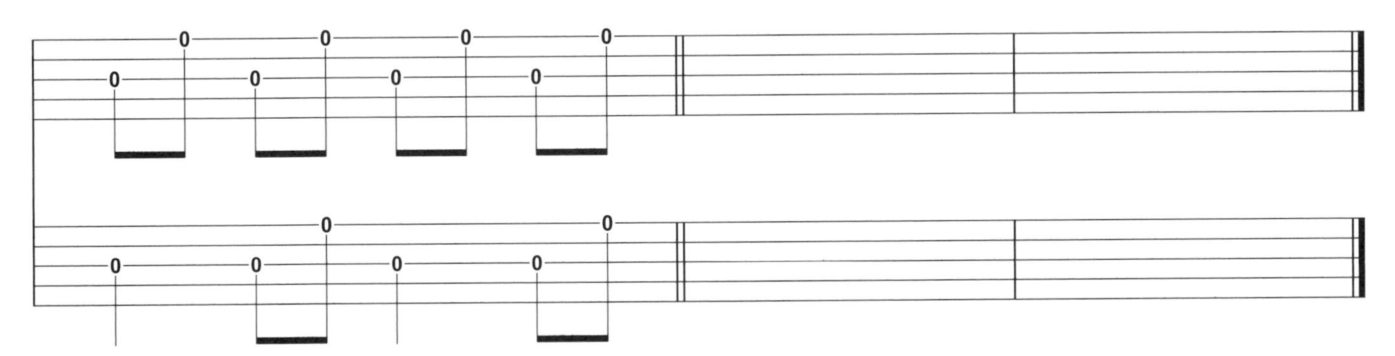

The following example shows that the melodic note can be a half-note in value, or three consecutive quarter notes (as indicated by the accent signs):

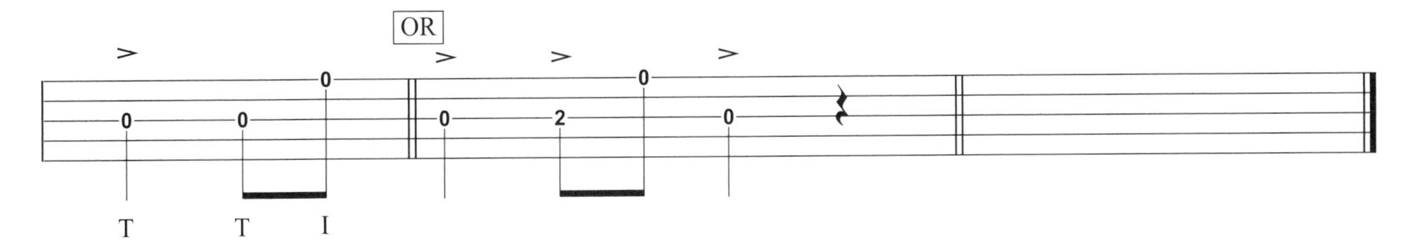

The thumb-lead style consists of three basic note sequences: the pinch, the broken pinch, and the thumb-lead roll.

The pinch is a technique where two strings are played at the same time, i.e., "pinching," the first and fifth strings together. This can be compared to the basic "chick" in the classic "boom–chick" pattern used in old-time country guitar styles, i.e., an alternation between a bass note and a chord on consecutive quarter note beats:

Pinch Pattern

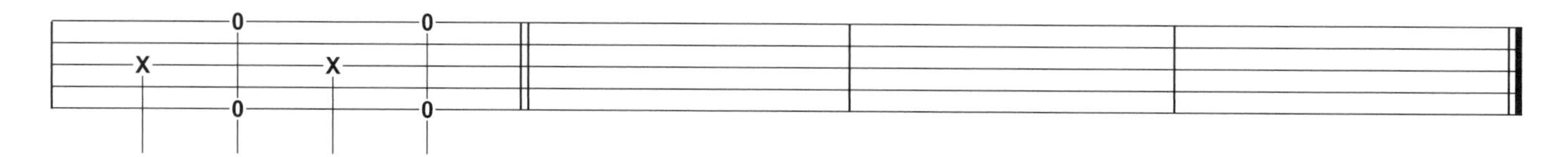

When the pinch is separated, or broken up, a broken pinch results:

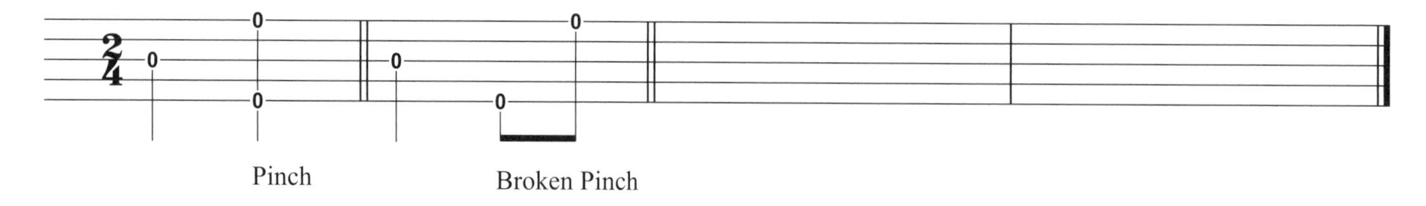

This leads to a type of 2-beat note sequence that I call the thumb-lead roll pattern (first example) which, in turn, leads to a 4-beat note sequence (second example):

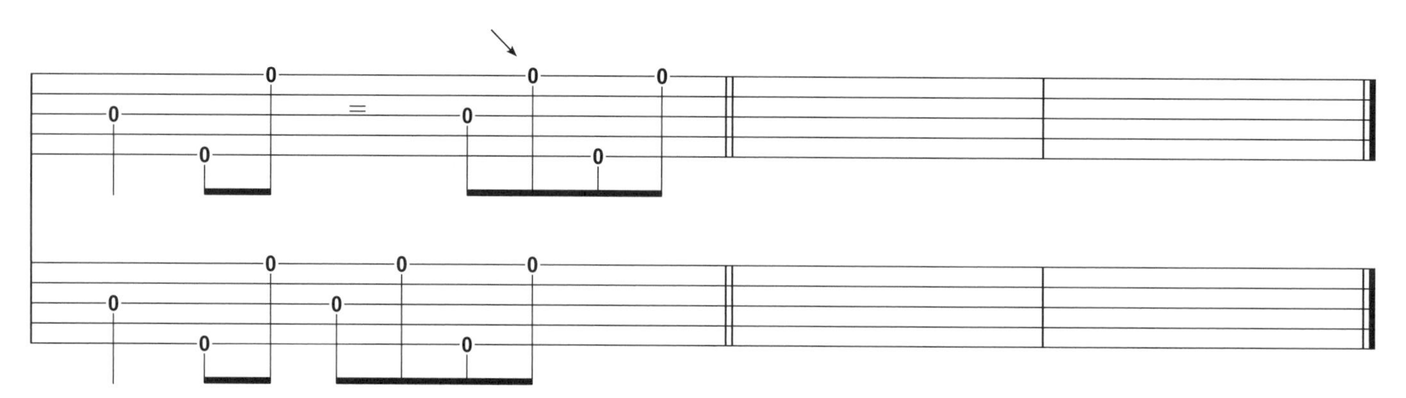

To add some variety, simply add some left hand articulations on beats 1 or 3.

While the thumb-lead style elements were used in many commercial recordings it was not necessarily quite like we are used to hearing it as the foundation of Scruggs-style banjo playing. Simply put, this is because melody notes are not incorporated within any type of "roll" or arpeggio pattern, which is the basis of Scruggs style.

PART II: STRING BAND TRANSCRIPTIONS OF SELECTED BACKUPS AND SOLOS

String bands didn't suddenly appear in the mid-1920s when field recordings began to occur, as late 19th century historic photos show that such ensemble configurations were common. While many string band musicians were self-taught, or learned from their local community musicians, there were many methods available for learning finger style banjo (for instance, by Frank Converse and S.S. Stewart), as well as sheet music by various commercial publishers and distributors. For instance, due to the centralized geographic location of Pittsburgh, the principal cargo hub at the head of the Ohio River, banjo methods could easily have been distributed down the Ohio Valley, into West Virginia, Kentucky, etc., for sale by local music stores, such as the Beckley Music Store in Beckley, West Virginia, or in any of the general merchandise stores run by the mill town owners or "company" stores run by coal mine or timber operators, who often sponsored community music courses for employees and their families; by furniture stores, where audio recordings and machines were usually sold; or direct, from mail order catalogs.

Now let's look at some backups and arrangements as recorded by various string band ensembles. You will see that parlor guitar technique influences much of their arranging style, or it was simply adapted as needed.

BANJO/CLAWHAMMER STYLE

The original banjo (clawhammer) style was frequently used in the old time music recordings to backup square dance and/or fiddle tunes; that style was also used by some solo vocalists (e.g., Buell Kazee). As an example, here is the basic backup used for the song *Banjo Sam*, as performed by Wilmer Watts:

Double C Tuning

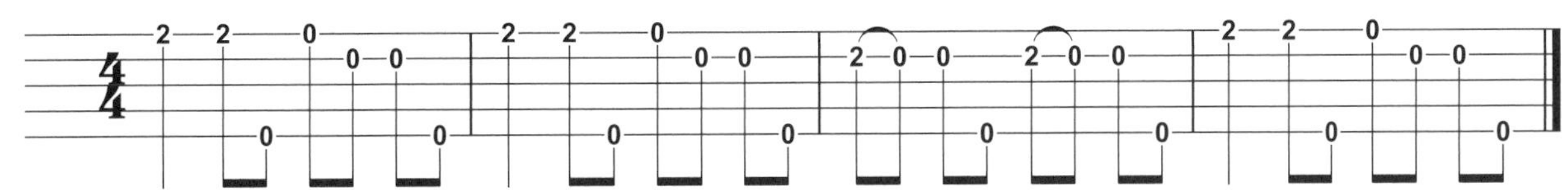

Here are some examples of songs where the clawhammer technique is used in the string band genre:

Banjo Sam
Wilmer Watts & the Lonely Eagles

Black-Eyed Susie
J.P. Nestor

John's Brown's Dream
Da Costa Woltz's Southern Broadcasters

Old Dan Tucker
Uncle Dave Macon

Possum Trot School Exhibition – Part 2
Stoneman's Blue Ridge Cornshuckers

Short Life of Trouble
Buell Kazee

Uncle Dave Macon

STRUMMING CHORDS

By the late 1920s the emergence of jazz, particularly the development of the jazz dance band, began to supersede the quaintness of the classic banjo style with the introduction of the louder 4-string tenor and plectrum banjos played in the plectrum style, used primarily as a rhythm instrument, to accompany and accent certain beats in the newer, faster dances, such as the Charleston and Fox Trot. In our context, the use of strummed chords was mainly found in the Memphis jug band backups.

Let's take a minute to look at the use of this technique. First of all, what a 5-string banjoist would have normally done would have been to detune the fifth string and reposition the slackened string to the left side of the bridge, thus lower in height than the remaining four long strings (this eventually led to the development of the similarly tuned four-string plectrum banjo, eliminating this necessity). Another option was simply to place the thumb on the fifth string, then strum down, for instance, with the middle finger and up with the index finger.

A "four to the bar" strumming sequence was also in use in songs such as *Piney Woods Girl* by Emmet Lundy and Ernest Stoneman and *Viola Lee Blues* by Cannon's Jug Stompers. This technique was apparently first introduced by New Orleans guitarist Bud Scott, who was one of the guitarists who played in cornetist Buddy Bolden's rhythm section in the then developing early jazz genre, ca. 1900. An interesting rhythmic variation was occasionally used, particularly by the jug bands in the Memphis area, where the banjoist would play chords only on beats 2 and 4, i.e., the backbeat, during certain parts of a song, e.g., during a solo by the jug player.

An obvious extension of this practice was to play a note on the downbeat, followed by three strummed chords, i.e., a common parlor guitar accompaniment technique. This was used, for example, on the song *Nine Pound Hammer* as performed by Frank Blevins & His Tar Heel Rattlers:

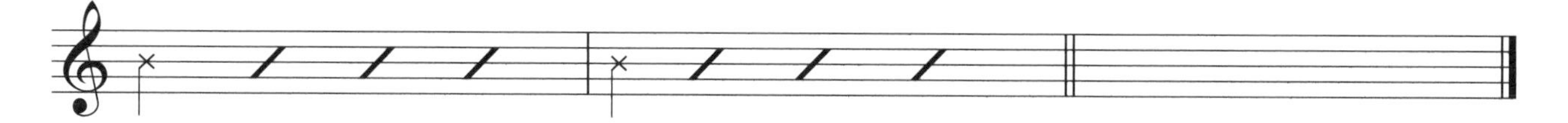

Sometimes the banjoist would be quite active, as in the song *Boll Weavil* recorded by W.A. Lindsey & Alvin Conder. In this recording a number of different strum patterns were employed:

Occasionally, some extra syncopated rhythmic strokes or triplet figures were added to the basic strummed backup. Here is a lead sheet example by the Memphis String Band on their interpretation of *He's in the Jailhouse Now*:

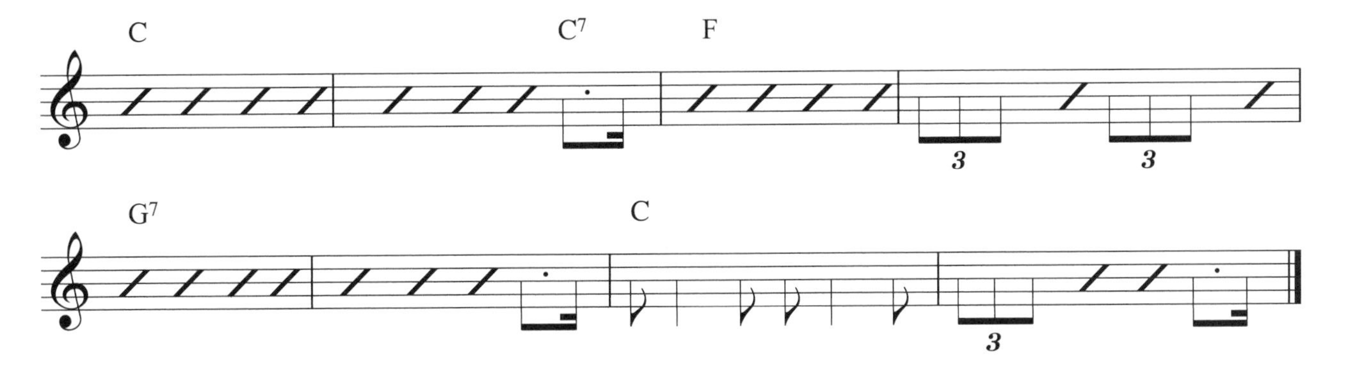

For the song *The Rooster's Crowing Blues* by Cannon's Jug Stompers, two additional techniques were employed: a tremoloed chord, as well as some picked notes outlining a D7 chord:

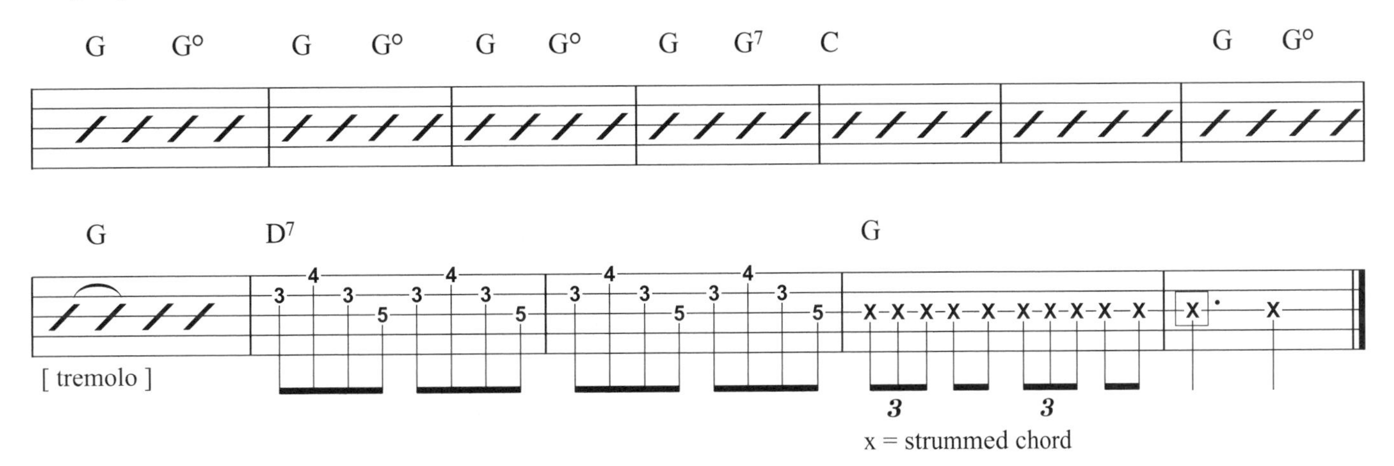

Quarter note strums were often subdivided rhythmically into pairs of eighth notes. In such cases the roots of the chords, or alternating bass notes, were played on beats 1 and 3. Here is an example:

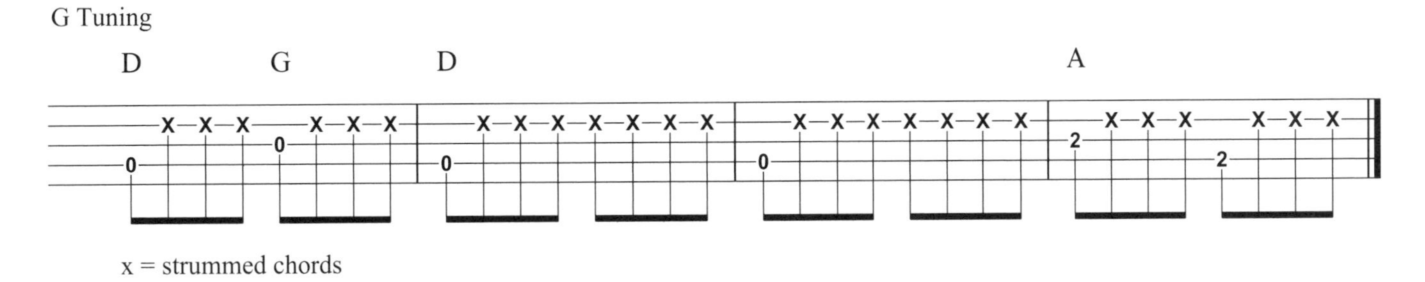

Here are a few songs from the string band genre where the banjoist performed his backup strumming only chords, often using "up the neck" chord inversions:

All Bound Down
Haywood County Ramblers

All I Got's Gone
Ernest Stoneman

Be Kind To A Man When He's Down
North Carolina Ridge Runners

I've Got No Honey Baby Now
Frank Blevins & His Tar Heel Rattlers

Old Aunt Betsy
Frank Blevins & His Tar Heel Rattlers

Sally Ann
Frank Blevins & His Tar Heel Rattlers

Shady Grove
Kentucky Thorobreds

They Don't Roost Too High For Me
Earl Johnson & His Clodhoppers

DOUBLING THE MELODY

Another technique used to back up string band songs was simply to "double" the melody, such as a fiddle player often did during vocals. Clawhammer banjoists often double the melody, or, at the very least, the principal melodic notes, driving a song along with the basic banjo rhythm.

Let's look at an example by Ernest V. Stoneman where the same 2-measure phrase is continually repeated as the backup to the fiddle tune *Sally Goodin*:

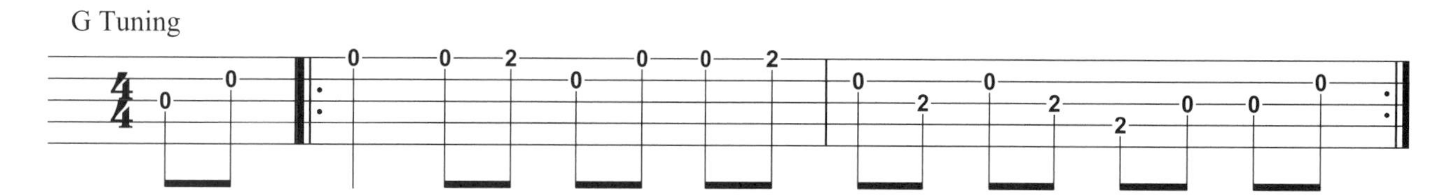

The following example comes from the song *Mule Get Up in the Alley*, as recorded by Cannon's Jug Stompers:

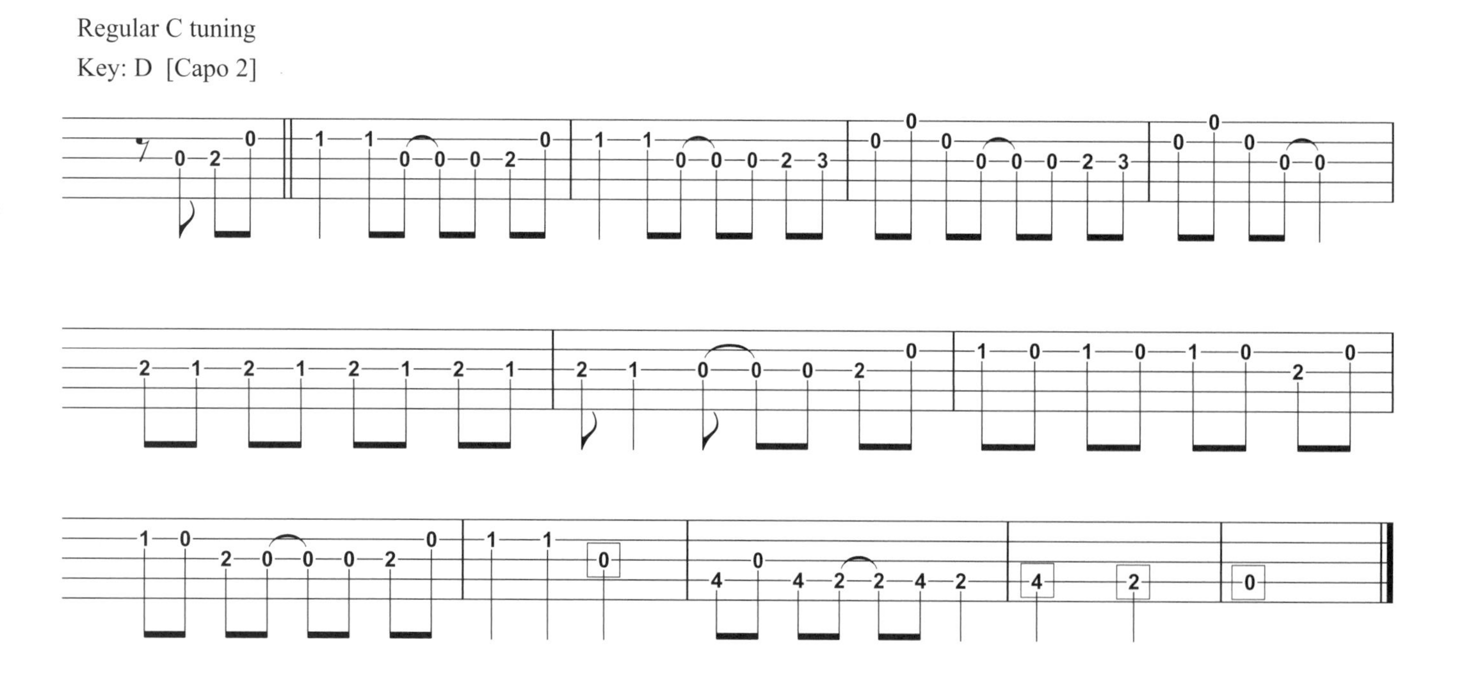

In the song *Glory Bye and Bye*, as recorded by Bela Lam and His Green County Singers, the introduction by the banjoist simply outlines the melody:

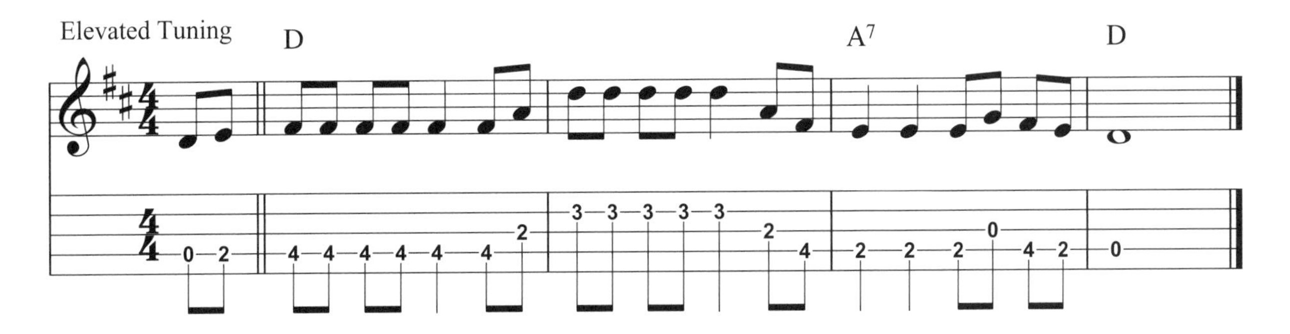

Next is an example for the song *Charley, He's A Good Old Man* as recorded by Gid Tanner and the Skillet Lickers (note that the doubling here occurs in the fifth and tenth positions instead of just the first position):

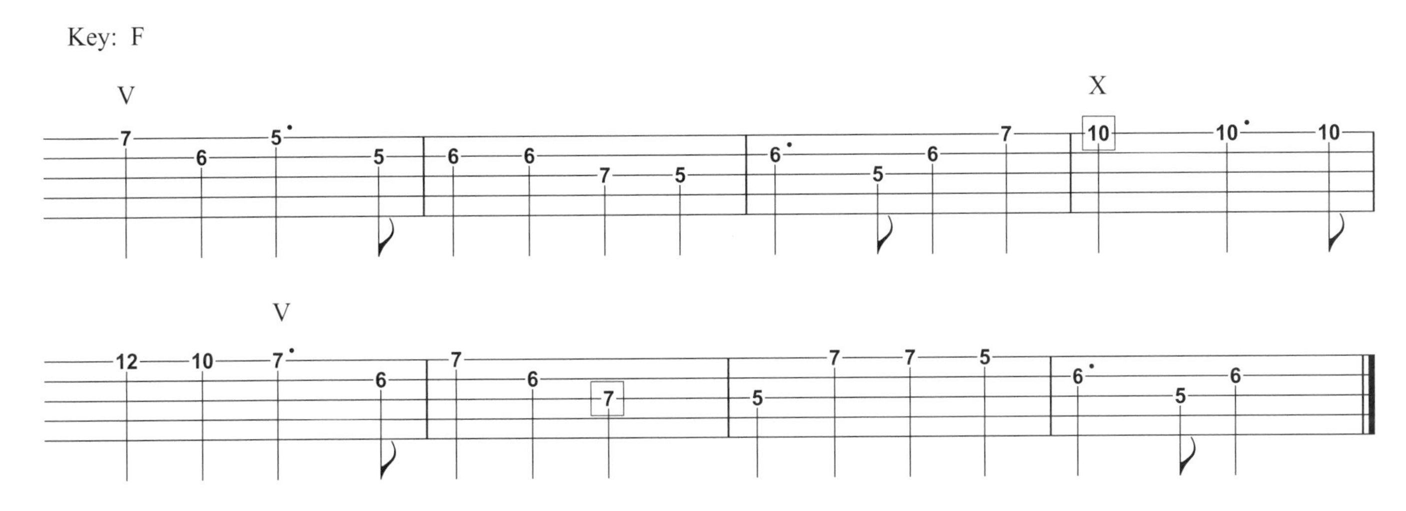

When the IV chord was played in the song *Boll Weavil* (F in that case) a syncopated two-string picking pattern was substituted "up the neck" instead of a strummed backup:

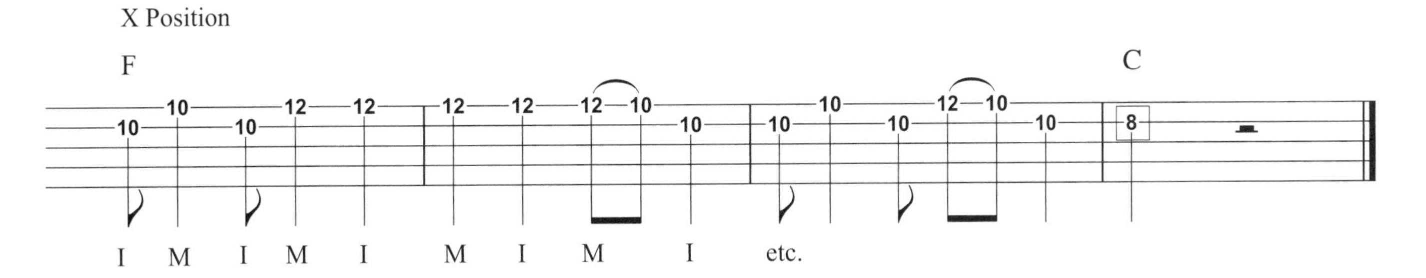

Next is an example of a backup, using either clawhammer or index-lead, using the basic banjo rhythm in the song *Your Blue Eyes Run Me Crazy*, as recorded by the Virginia Coon Hunters (once again note that most of the accompaniment is played "up the neck" out of the fifth position):

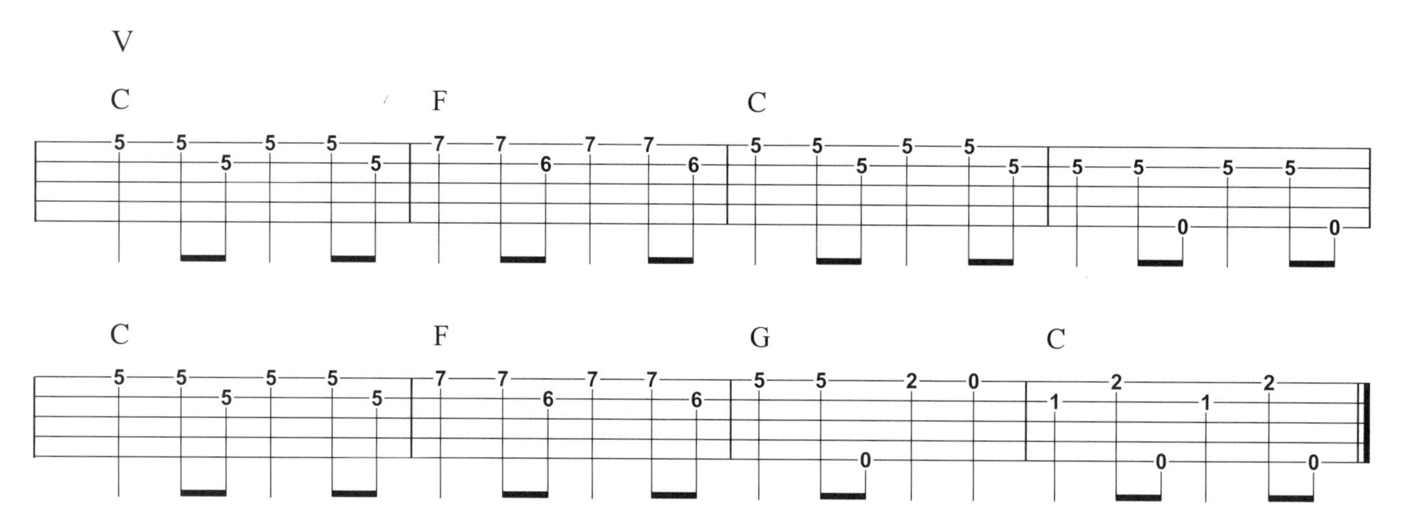

Here are some additional string band songs featuring this doubling technique as the principal banjo backup feature:

Billy Grimes the Rover
The Shelor Family

Round Town Gals
Ernest V. Stoneman

Careless Love
Ernest V. Stoneman and His Dixie Mountaineers

He Is Coming After Me
Ernest V. Stoneman and His Dixie Mountaineers

He Was Nailed to the Cross for Me
Ernest V. Stoneman and His Dixie Mountaineers

It's Sinful to Flirt
Ernest V. Stoneman and His Dixie Mountaineers

The Old Man and the Burglar
Ernest V. Stoneman and His Dixie Mountaineers

Sandy River Belle
Dad Blackard's Moonshiners

The Unlucky Road to Washington
Ernest V. Stoneman and His Dixie Mountaineers

When the Redeemed Are Gathering In
Ernest V. Stoneman and His Dixie Mountaineers

THUMB-LEAD STYLE

The thumb-lead style has several possible evolutionary scenarios:

[1] reversing the index-lead double-thumb figure;

[2] borrowing the thumb-index two-finger style of country blues guitarists; or

[3] rearranging notes in first position that were played in index-lead or clawhammer style to a closed position, e.g., an F chord shape at the third position.

If you **reverse the index-lead movements** you basically end up using the thumb to play notes on the beat. Here is an example showing that comparison:

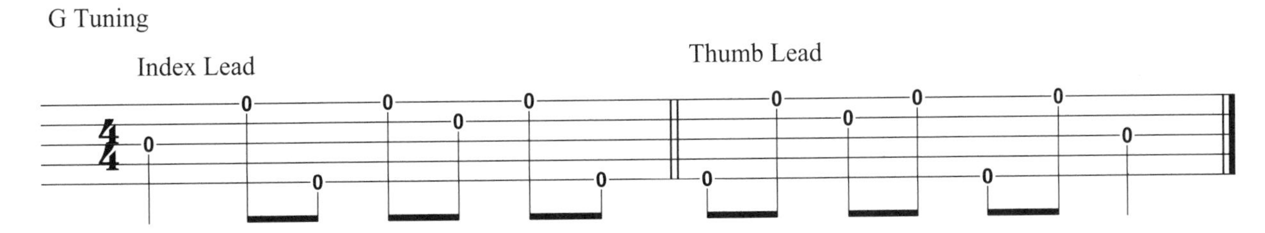

In fact, the backup for the fiddle tune *Billy In The Low Ground*, as recorded by Burnett & Rutherford in November 1927, uses the reverse note sequence, so let's look at the first eight measures of that backup:

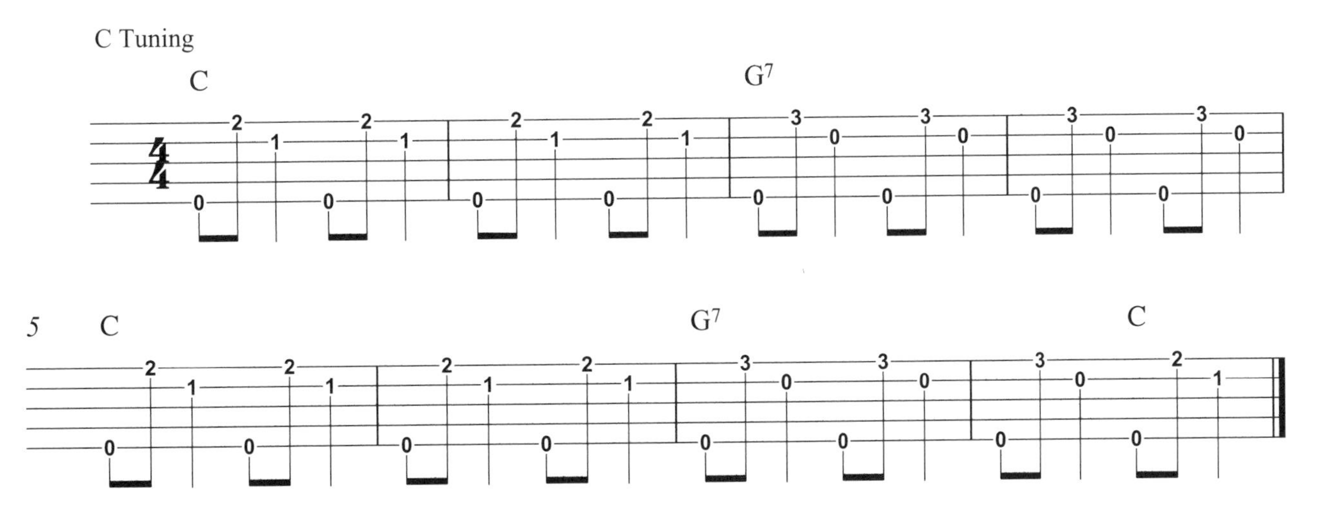

In the second section of this song an F chord is used. Here is how that is played:

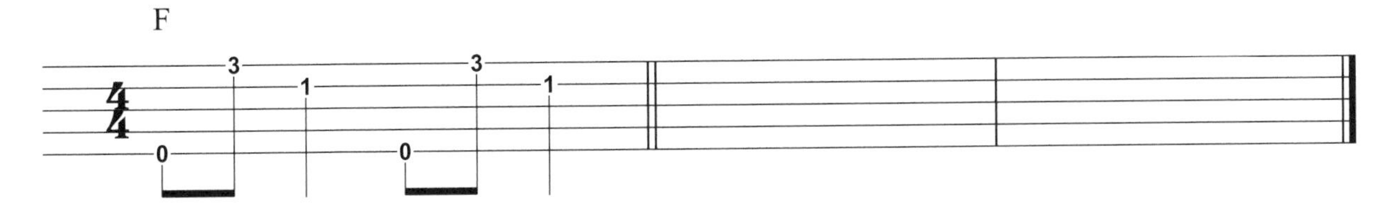

You could easily play those chords in fifth position. Here are the fingerings you would use for the C, F and G7 chords (the right hand fingerings necessarily change from TIT to MIT that results, by necessity, from thumb-lead to guitar style technique):

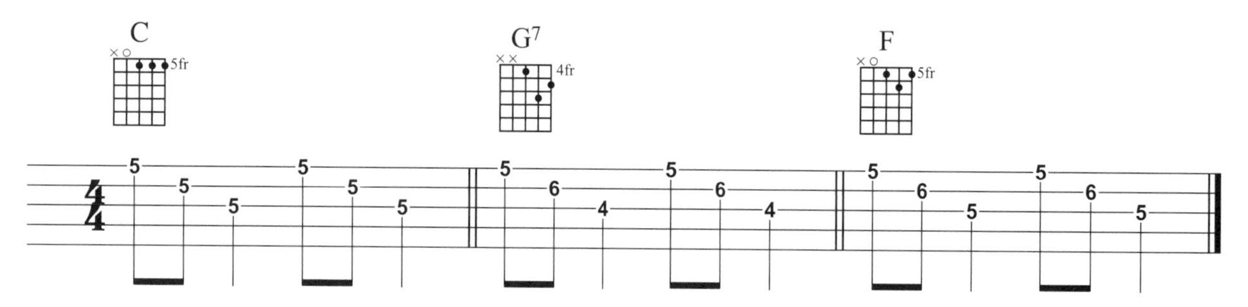

This arrangement also features a short strummed chord pattern which replaces the initial measure of each two-measure phrase. Here is how that looks:

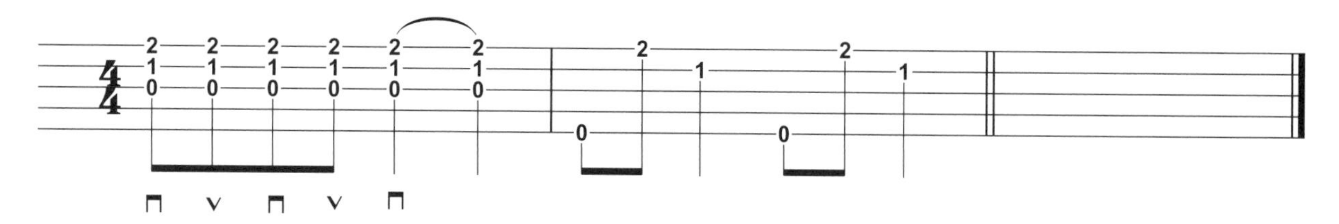

The second scenario is that thumb lead style was adapted from the emerging country blues guitar performance style based on using only the thumb and the index finger to play, including **pinches** that I discussed earlier (which is not possible to play in the original "banjo style"):

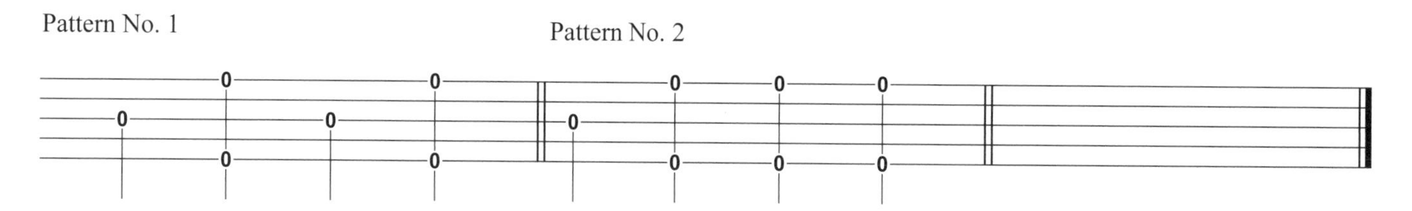

Of course, open G tuning is popular in the country blues guitar genre. When this tuning is used the highest four strings of the blues guitar matches the open G tuning used in 5-string banjo (referred to as "elevated tuning" in the 19th century banjo methods, i.e., the fourth string of the banjo was raised, or elevated, in pitch by a whole step).

The third scenario is to play a note sequence played in first position using index-lead to, say, an F chord shape at the third position; that leaves no alternative but to use thumb lead (although you could also use IM for TI in the latter example, adhering to the classic banjo three-finger technique):

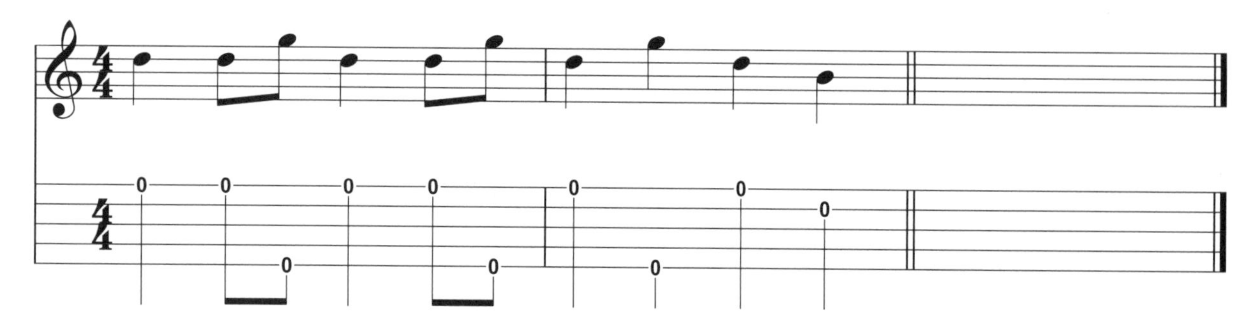

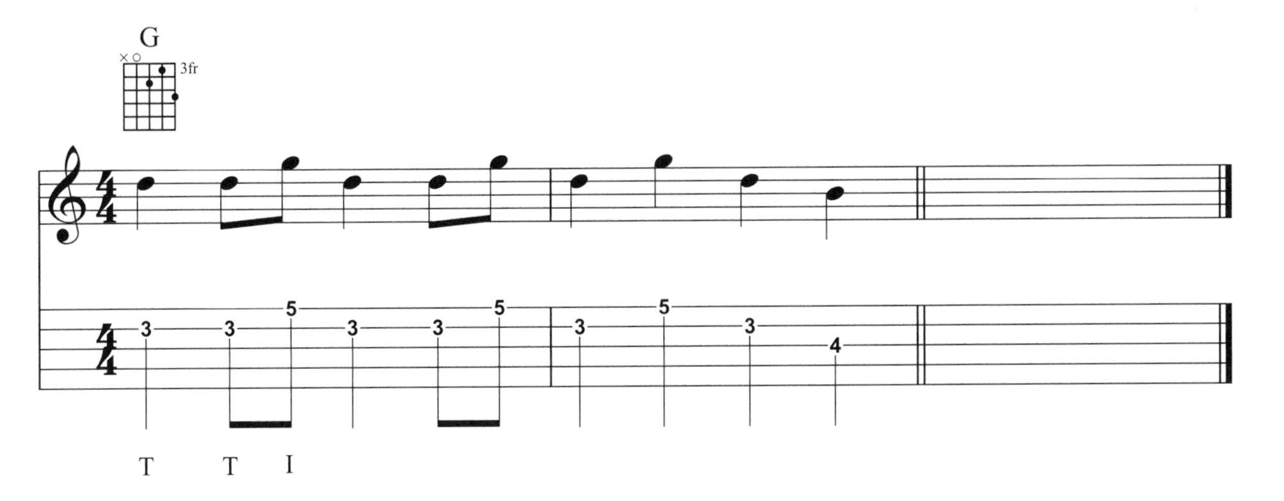

The following string band songs used Pinch Pattern No. 1 as their basic backup technique:

> *Going to Germany*
> Cannon's Jug Stompers
>
> *Last Gold Dollar*
> Ephriam Woodie & the Henpecked Husbands
>
> *The Prisoner's Lament*
> Ernest V. Stoneman and His Dixie Mountaineers

Here are some songs where Pinch Pattern No. 2 was used as the basic backup technique:

> *All Go Hungry Hash House*
> Ernest V. Stoneman and His Dixie Mountaineers
>
> *Are You Angry With Me Darling*
> Blue Ridge Highballers
>
> *Down on the Banks of the Ohio*
> Ernest V. Stoneman and His Dixie Mountaineers
>
> *I Remember Calvary*
> Ernest V. Stoneman and His Dixie Mountaineers
>
> *Watchman Ring That Bell*
> Ernest V. Stoneman and His Dixie Mountaineers
>
> *We Parted At the River*
> Ernest V. Stoneman and His Dixie Mountaineers

Four-beat backup patterns are often repeated as a principal backup. For instance, when you combine a thumb-lead roll followed by a pinch, I call this a roll-and-pinch pattern. The song *The Old Hat*, as recorded by the Leake County Revelers, uses that note sequence:

Roll-Pinch Pattern

G

In the song *C&O Whistle*, recorded by the Fruit Jar Guzzlers in March 1928, the thumb-lead roll leads to a flowing backup pattern:

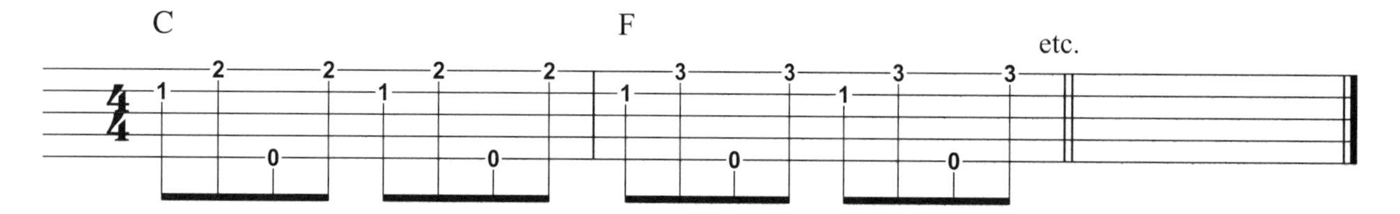

Mixed 4-beat backups. It is not unusual for two related backup techniques to be used in one song, perhaps one technique used for the verse and the other for the chorus or instrumental break. For instance, in the song *Tar and Feathers*, recorded on November 29, 1939, in Memphis, TN, by Fisher Hendley, the basic pinch pattern and the roll-and-pinch pattern are both used in his backup:

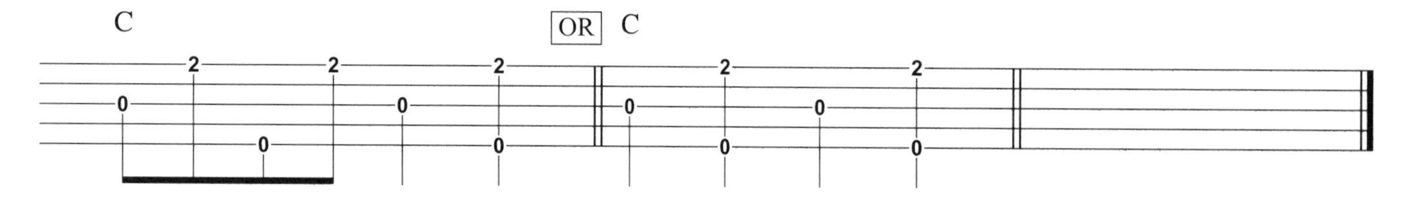

The song *Chain Gang Special*, as recorded by Watts & Wilson, uses either the thumb-lead roll or a pinch-and-roll pattern:

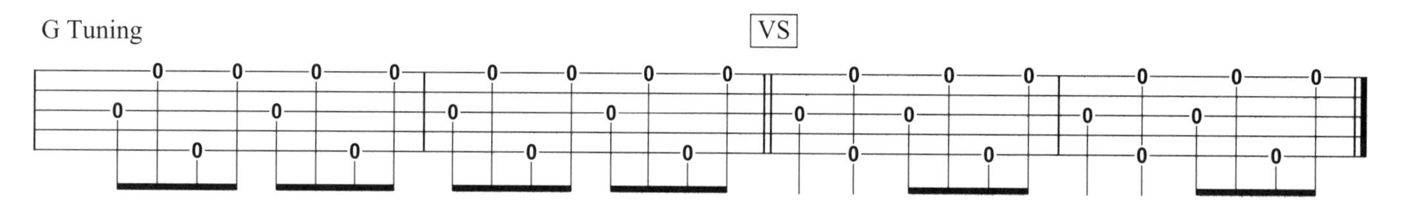

The banjoist with the Kissinger Brothers used all of the pinch patterns we have been discussing so far in their recorded version of the song *Kentucky Bootlegger*:

Three Backup Patterns:

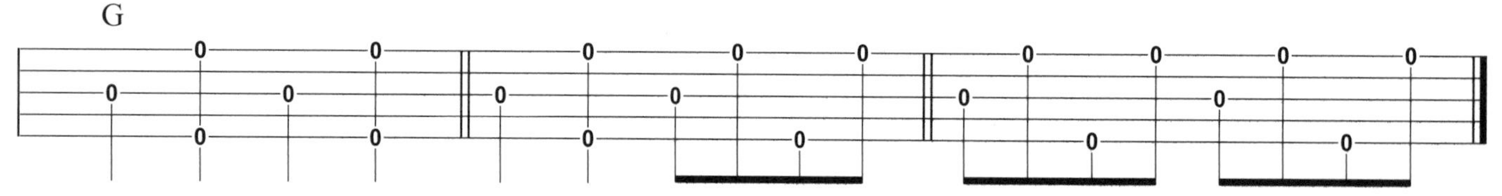

2-MEASURE COMBINATION PATTERNS

Songs in Common time often are based on two or four measure musical phrases. Let's now look at a few examples where thumb-lead patterns were combined as a 2-measure backup pattern. The following two-measure pattern was used in the song *Take Me Back to the Sweet Sunny South*, as recorded by DaCosta Woltz's Southern Broadcasters in May 1927, i.e., the same pattern was used for each chord change:

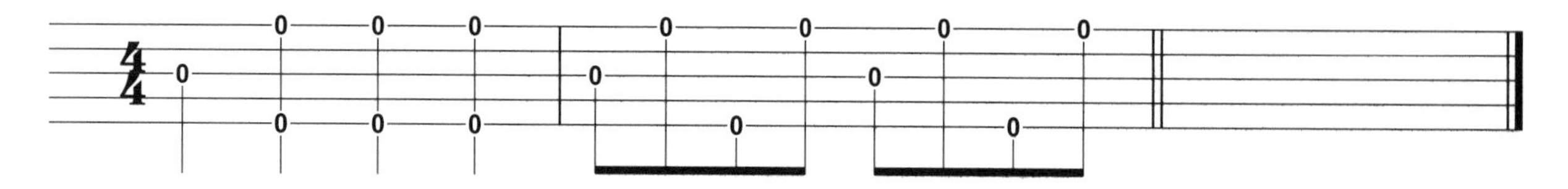

Here is another commonly used two-measure thumb-lead backup pattern:

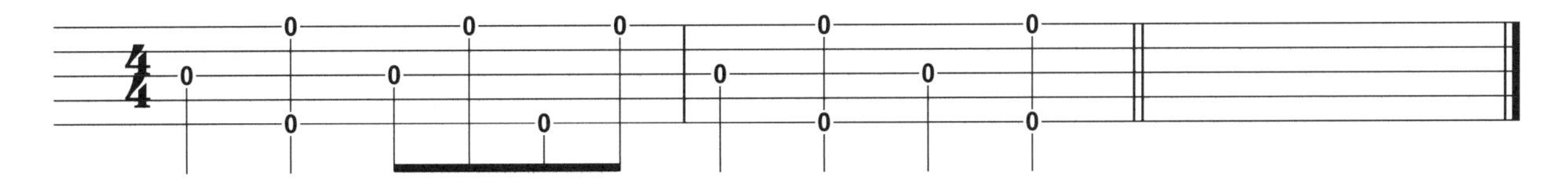

Let's look at another song recorded by Fisher Hendley. In this particular backup, used in his recording of *Weave Room Blues*, he used three distinct backup patterns over the tonic C chord at different points:

Regular C Tuning

Three Backup Patterns:

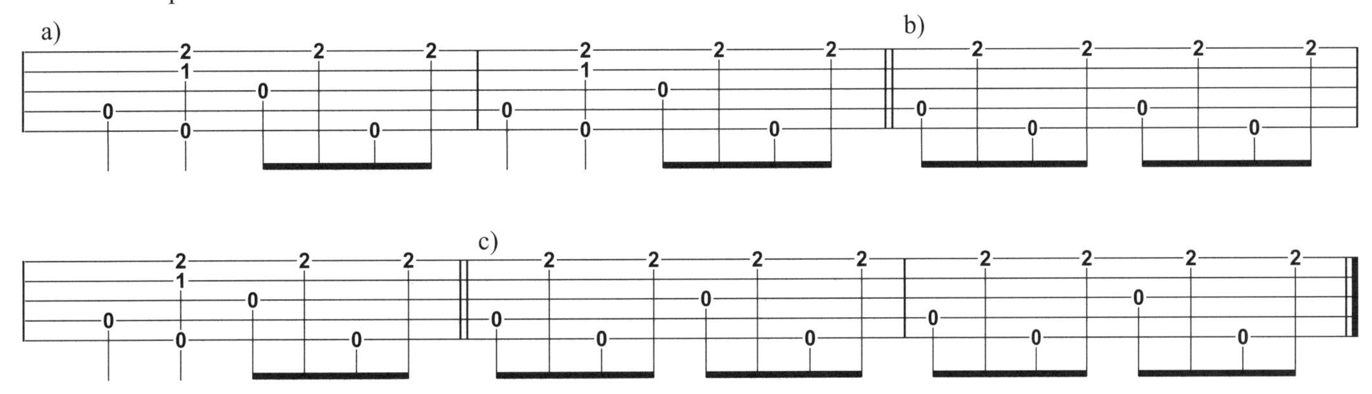

Over the IV chord he used the following patterns:

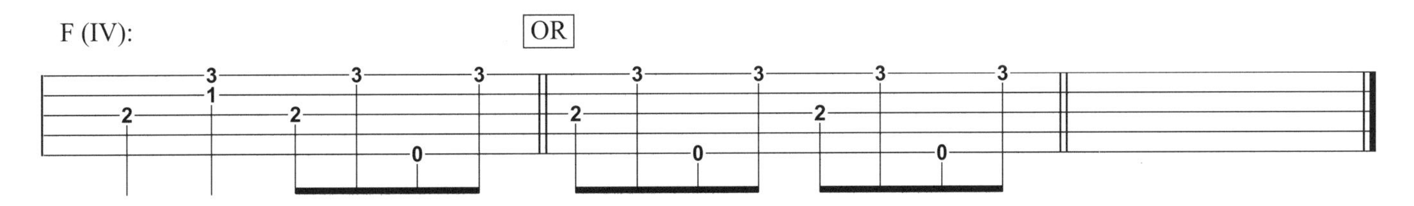

And, over the V7 chord, Hendley used these patterns:

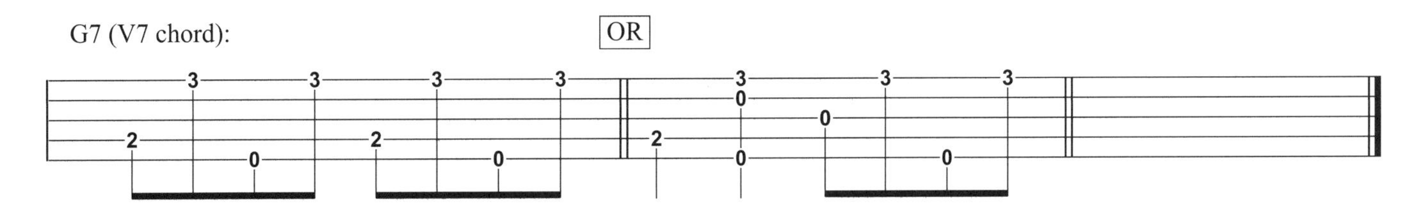

As you can see in this backup Hendley used a variety of backup techniques instead of just one or two basic patterns throughout, as shown in the earlier examples.

Let's now look at a song that is modal-based, as well as crooked. The tuning used for *Oh Molly Dear*, as recorded by B.F. Shetlon, is G Mountain Minor:

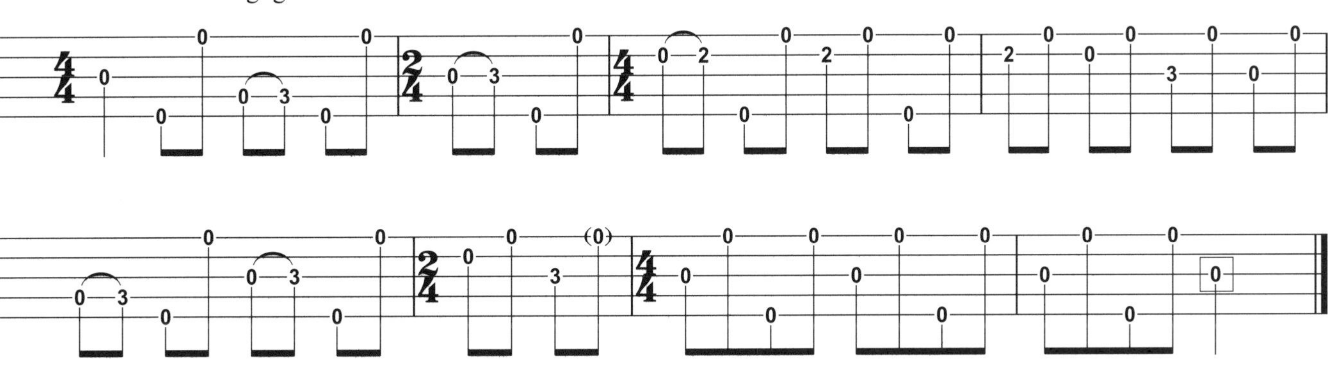

GUITAR STYLE

As I have shown so far, a lot of the 5-string banjo backups in the string band genre can be fairly basic in nature. As there was often a guitarist in such ensembles sharing backup responsibilities, they continued to play their traditional rhythmic patterns and walking bass lines, as those notes were lower in range than those available on the banjo, thus stronger in volume (which, in turn, acted as a harmonic anchor for the ensemble).

Charlie Poole. As I mentioned earlier, the ragtime banjo style was the one that Charlie Poole loved to listen to and play (particularly the "sides" recorded by Fred Van Eps, father of the 7-string jazz guitar wizard George VanEps). Poole apparently learned to play that style from a local banjoist in the North Carolina piedmont (where Poole lived and worked from time to time in the textile mills), probably Daner Johnson, who was fluent in the "guitar style" 3-finger technique. In the tried-and-true folk tradition Charlie Poole would have also learned songs and other techniques from banjo players that he encountered during his numerous "ramblings," or that he "caught" at vaudeville shows, various local entertainments, social gatherings, etc.

Poole rarely soloed on any of the numerous recordings that he made with his North Carolina Ramblers; it is known, however, that he did record some banjo solos with piano accompaniment (in the classic banjo style tradition) but his record company chose to not issue them as they conflicted with the marketing and commercial success of his string band "sides." All of the songs and instrumental numbers that were issued featuring Charlie Poole and his group were recorded in the keys of D, F, A, G or C. Photos of Poole often show him fingering an F chord shape up the neck (i.e., the key of C in that fingerboard position) or the C chord shape at the nut. As the fourth string is not "stopped" in those photographs it indicates that his banjo was tuned to the standard C tuning. However, Poole probably would have also been fluent playing in the keys of B flat and E flat, as they are commonly used keys in the classic banjo literature.

Many banjo backups in string band music combine the "guitar style" and, occasionally, elements of thumb-lead style as the situation warrants. For instance, the equivalent of a thumb-lead pinch pattern in classic banjo is the following:

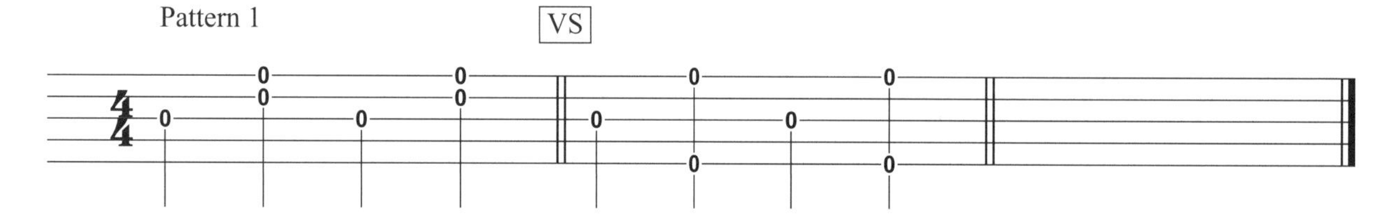

You might recall that the first measure of Dobson's *Little Mary Polka* used this pattern.

Occasionally, the double stop on beats 2 and 4 will be replaced by an **index finger strum**, as in the backup for the song *She's A Flower From the Fields of Alabama* recorded by Rutherford, Moore & Burnett. In addition, that recording features several different guitar style backup licks, so here they are over a C chord:

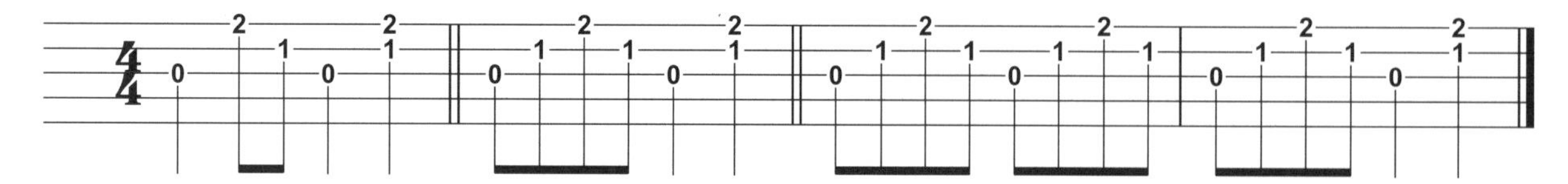

The backup for the song *Homebrew Rag*, as recorded by the Roanoke Jug Band, uses Pattern 1 "up the neck" over G, C, D and G chord inversions:

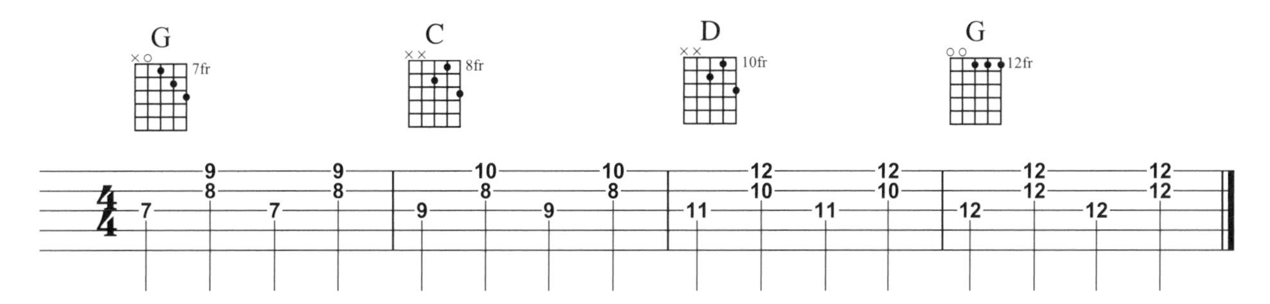

At other times the backup for that song consists of the following broken arpeggios, using either TIMI or TIM:

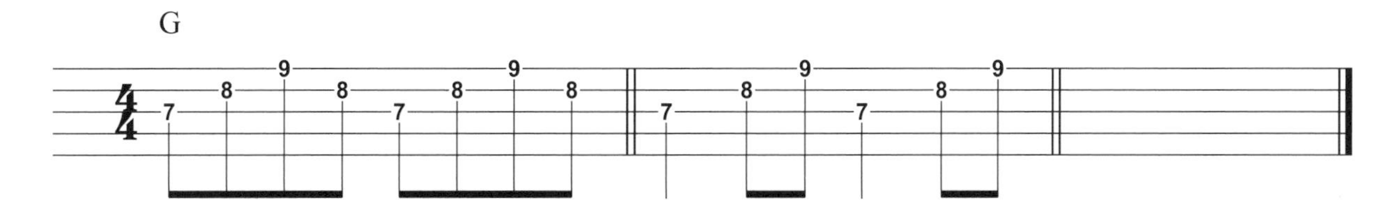

The song, *Once I Loved a Railroad Flagman*, was recorded by Frank Jenkins & His Pilot Mountaineers (see related information later under the section on Frank Jenkins); it is a two chord song, the same chord outlines being used throughout the arrangement (note in particular the fingering for the D7 chord):

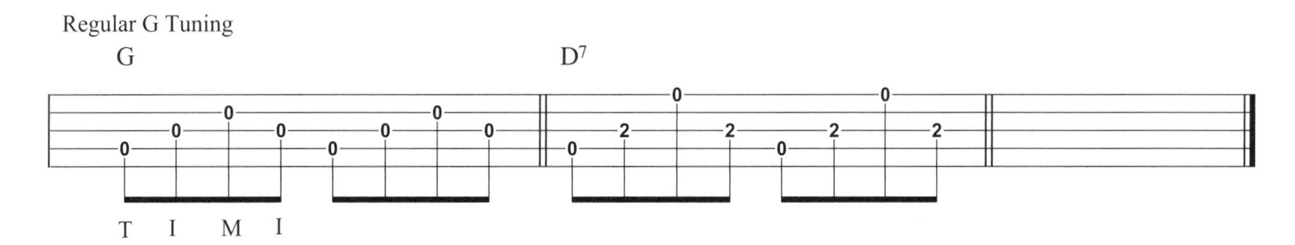

Several variations are used in the banjo backup to the song *Been on the Job Too Long* (aka *Brady and Duncan*) as recorded by Wilmer Watts and the Lonely Eagles. Here, the basic "guitar" style pinch is broken up:

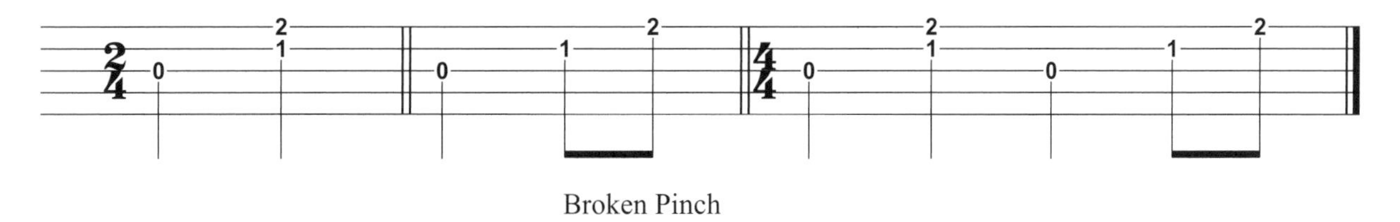

This pattern was occasionally reversed:

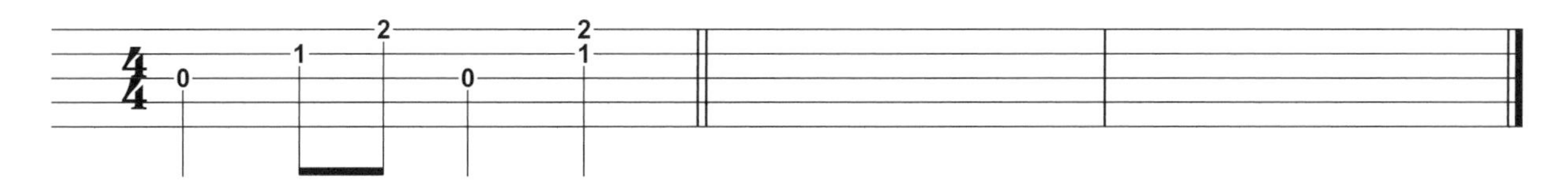

Next, a basic pinch pattern is followed by a TIMI arpeggio figure, sort of a pinch-and-roll combination:

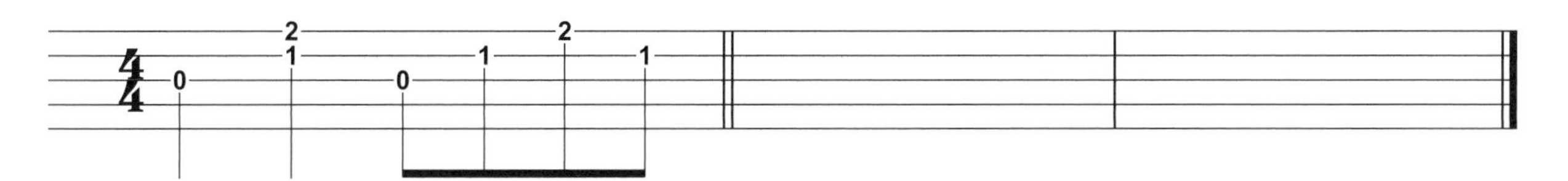

Over a four-measure phrase this figure is repeated followed in the fourth measure by two pinch patterns using an alternating bass note pattern:

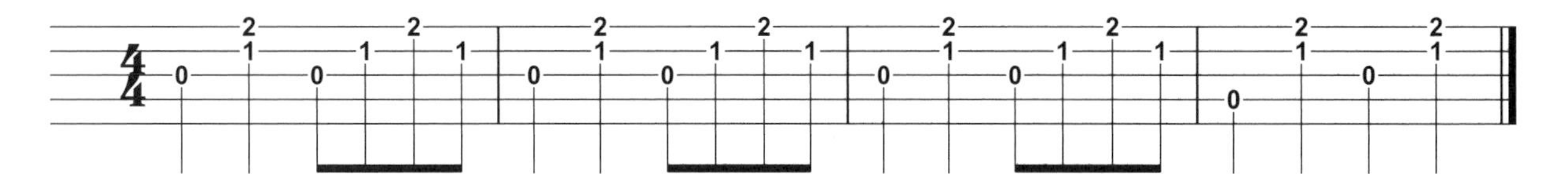

Consecutive TIMI arpeggios are also used, similar to a repeated thumb-lead roll pattern:

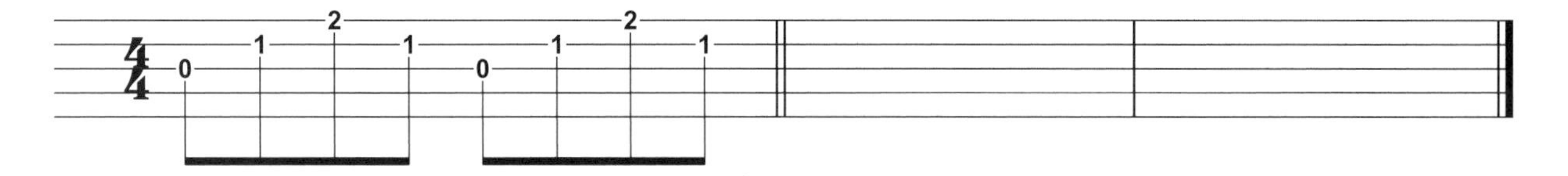

Finally, when the F (IV) chord is played the following syncopated figure was used:

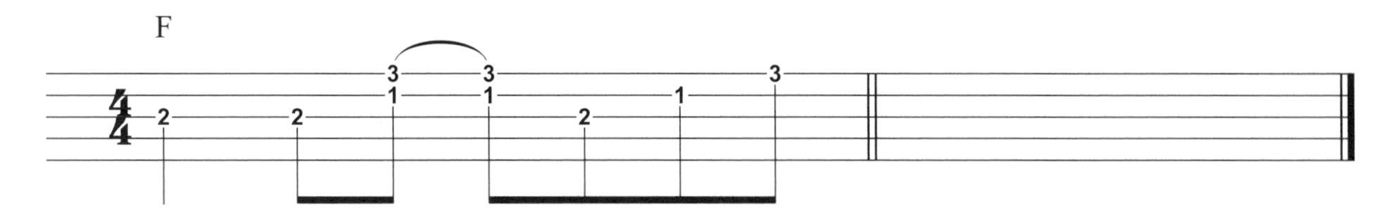

As mentioned earlier, the melody of a song was often "doubled" by the banjoist. Here are the first eight bars of the basic melody for *Cotton Mill Blues*, as recorded by Wilmer Watts and the Lonely Eagles, utilizing that technique:

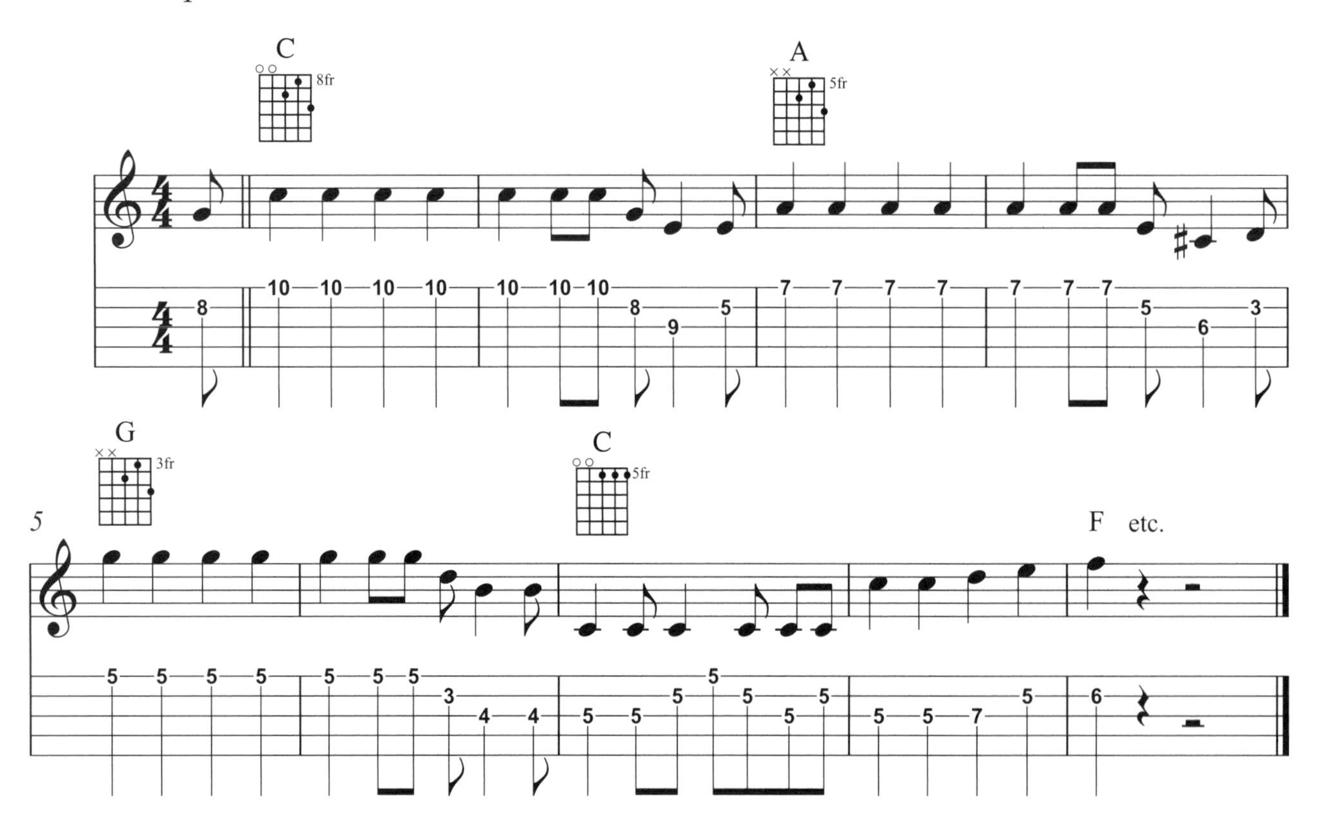

Note that the last note of measures 2 and 4 is where you need to shift chord positions.

Also, in measure 7 a forward-backward roll is used:

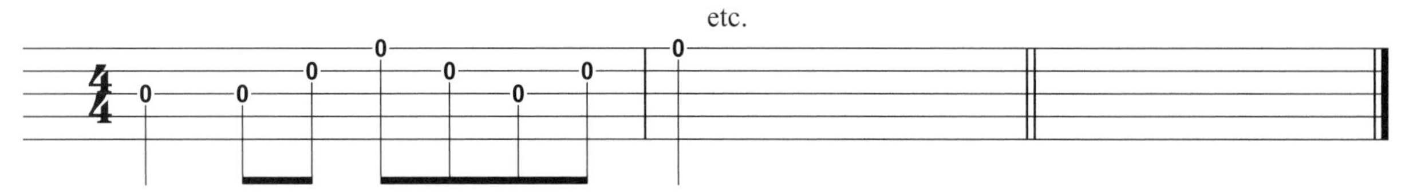

Here is how that pattern was used in the concluding coda:

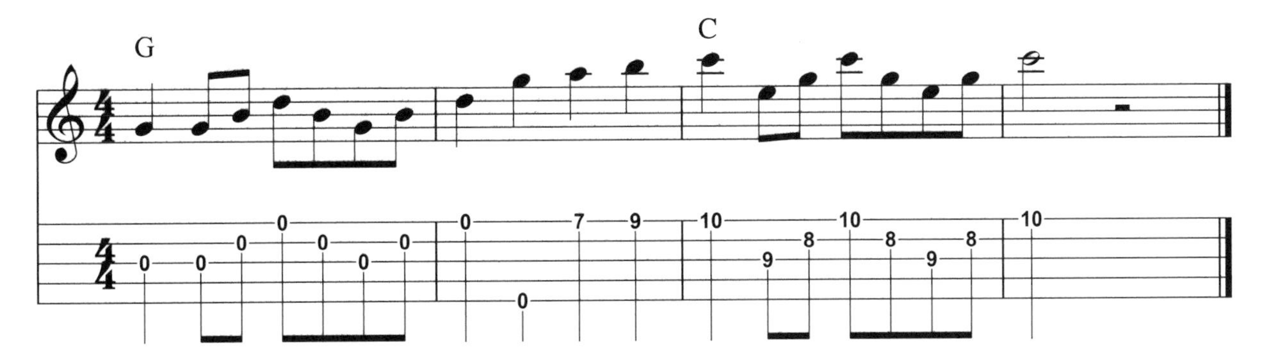

The next song, *If Tonight Should End the World*, as recorded by Bela Lam and His Green County Singers, features the use of several arpeggio patterns on the inside strings. For instance, about a minute into the recording the following arpeggio is used over the D and G chords:

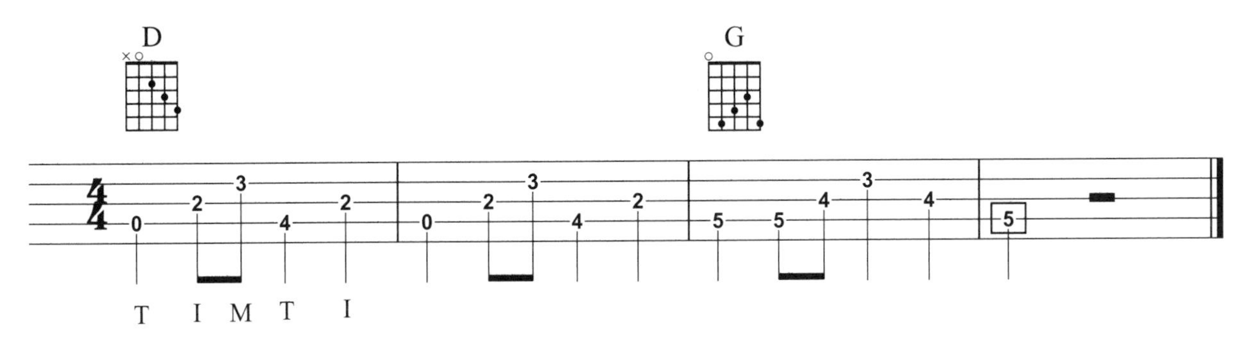

Around the 1:50" mark this V-I chord change is then played in the following manner:

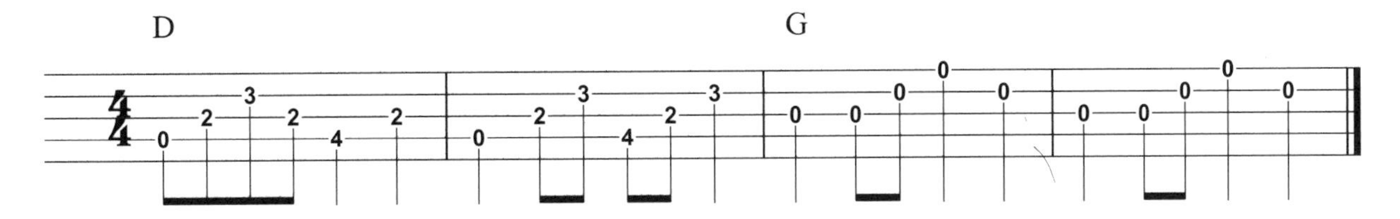

There is yet another way to play those two chords (at around the 2:08" mark):

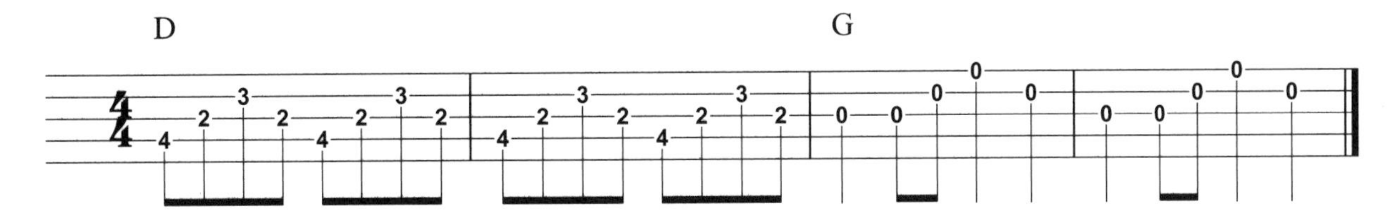

The following is the backup pattern used throughout the song over the different chord changes (which was also used in their backup in the recording of the song, *Crown Him*):

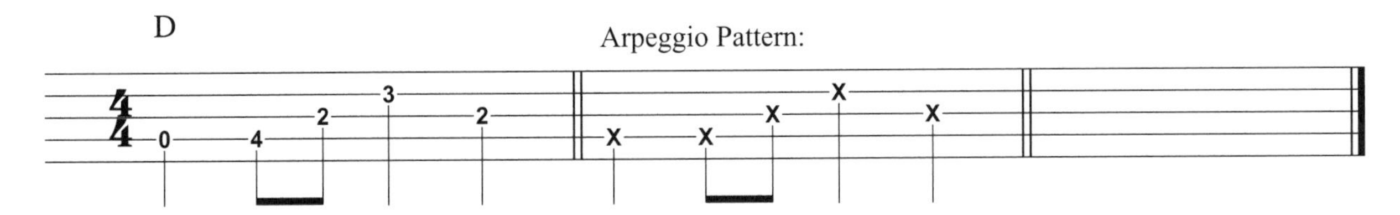

Here is the closing coda:

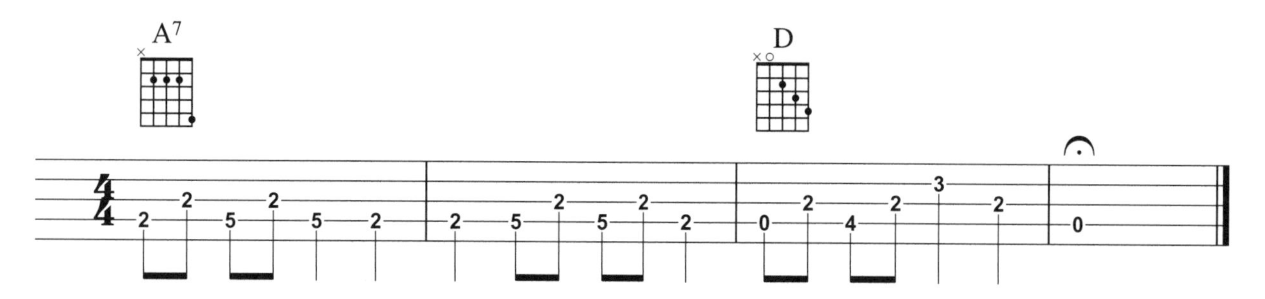

The backup to the song *The Married Man*, recorded by Emory Arthur in the spring of 1931, uses a reversed thumb-lead figure over the tonic chord and use of an arpeggio pattern over the V chord, D Major. Here are those note sequences:

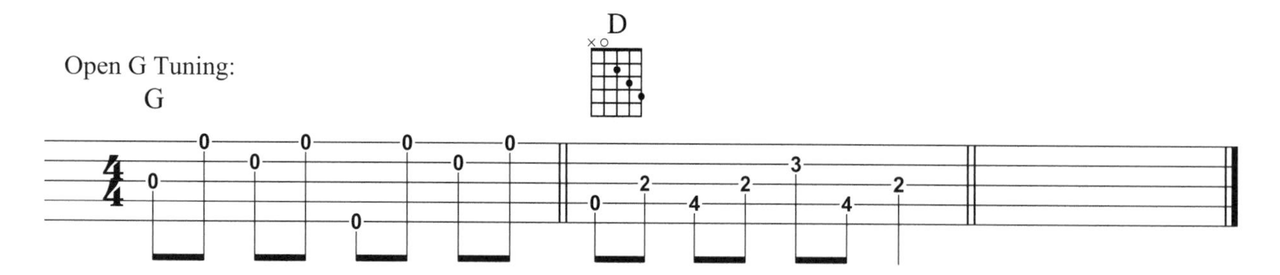

When chords are played in closed positions in that song the following pattern is employed, i.e., thumb-lead and the reverse roll:

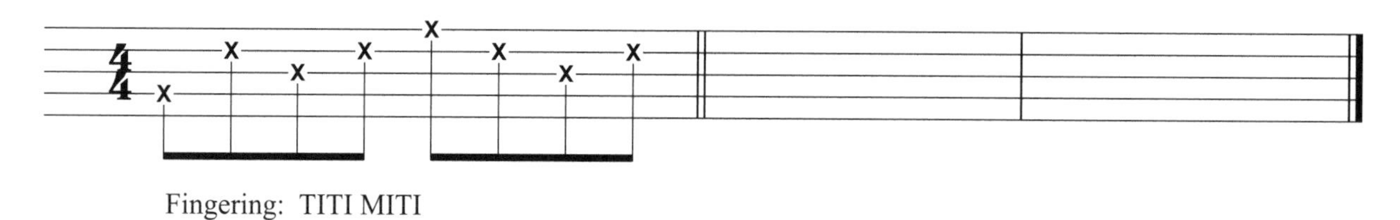

That arpeggio pattern was also used in the song *There's a Treasure Up In Heaven*, also recorded by Emory Arthur during the period April-May 1931. Here it is:

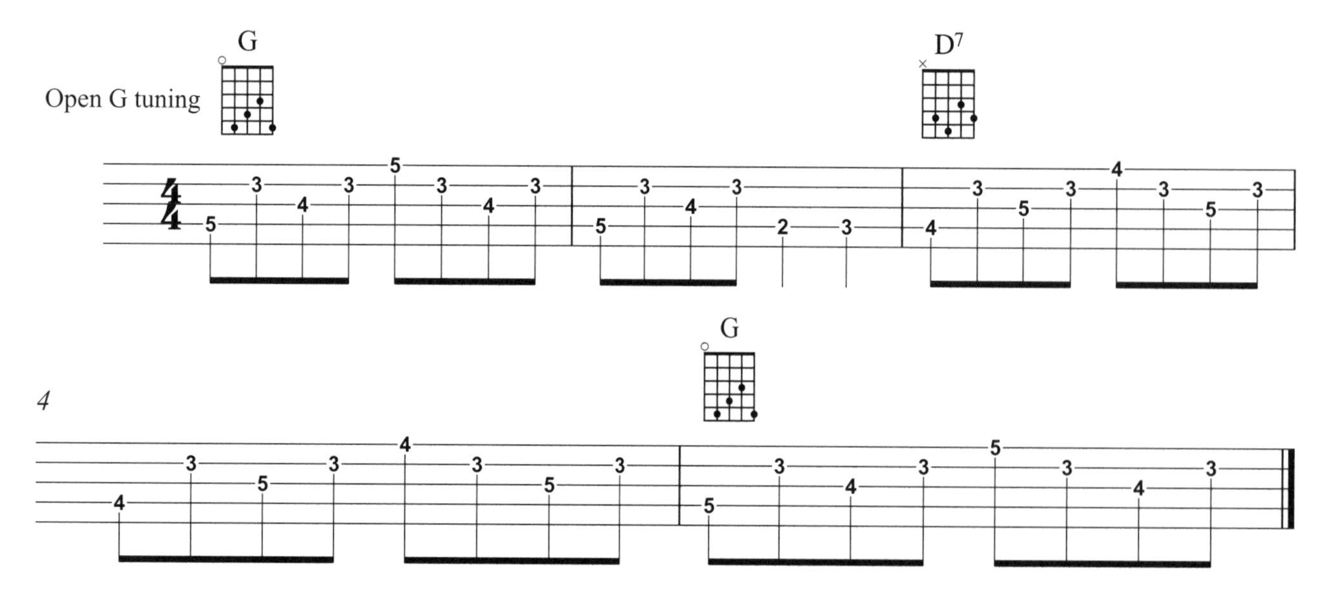

If the first and last measures in G are played in open (first) position then it resembles a Scruggs-style roll pattern (this backup pattern was just outlined in *The Married Man*):

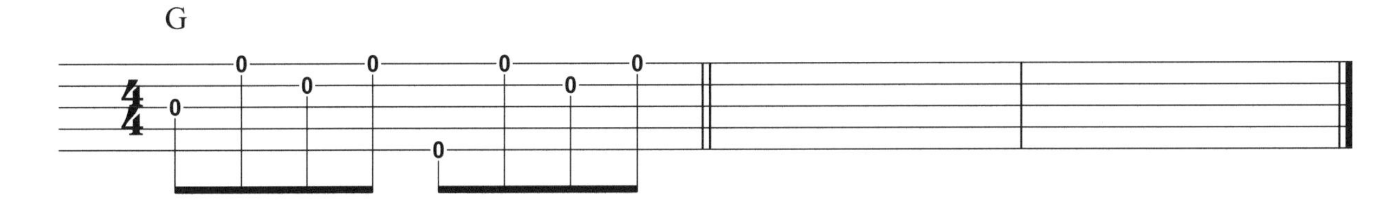

The next song, *Curly Headed Woman*, was recorded by Burnett & Rutherford in the key of E using the open E tuning of g# E G# B E. I will discuss this tuning, as well as open D tuning, in more detail later on when I present a number of instrumental breaks and solos by Uncle Dave Macon and Frank Jenkins. This is a crooked song, in that eleven measures are used instead of the expected twelve; however, as two measures are in 6/4 time in the end it actually works out all right.

Curly Headed Woman is basically played in thumb-lead style that, due to the open E tuning, requires minimal work by the left hand:

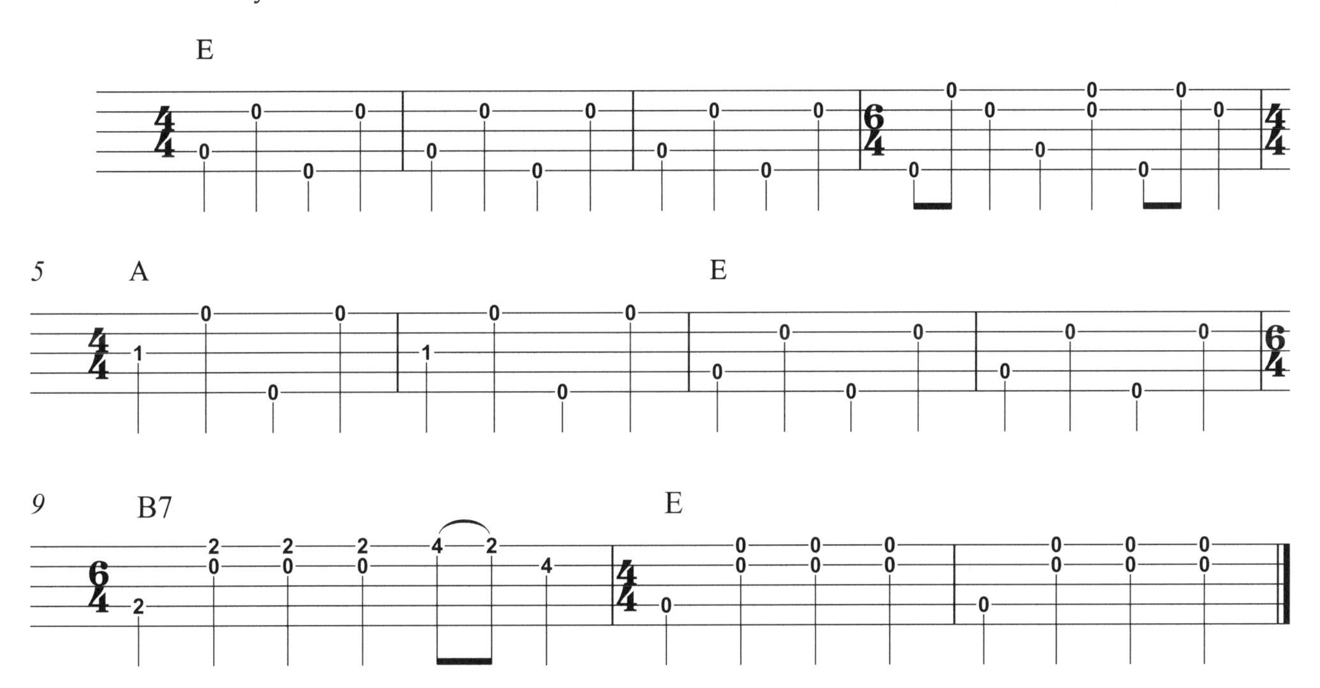

Throughout the song, several related open string rhythmic variations are used to vary the backup:

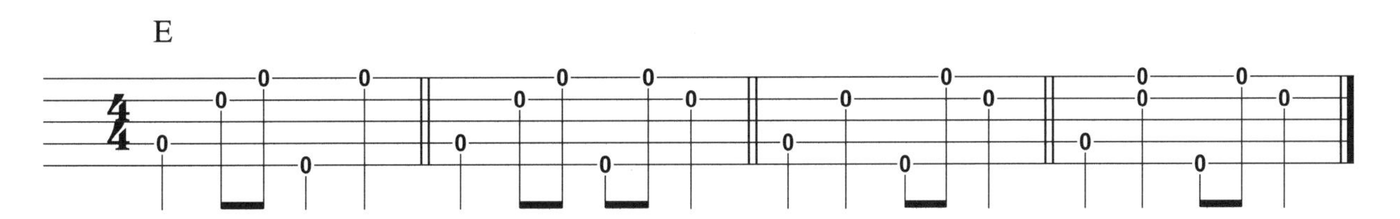

We will come back to these variations later on when I discuss the song *Baptist Shout* by Frank Jenkins.

The next backup is for the traditional song *Ground Hog*, here as recorded by Jack Reedy & His Walker Mountain String Band. The first half of the arrangement consists of two pinch patterns followed by an arpeggio-like figure to form two-measure phrases (note the repeated notes on the first string). This backup contains elements of the thumb-lead style because the thumb plays most of the notes which are positioned on beats 1 and 3 of each measure:

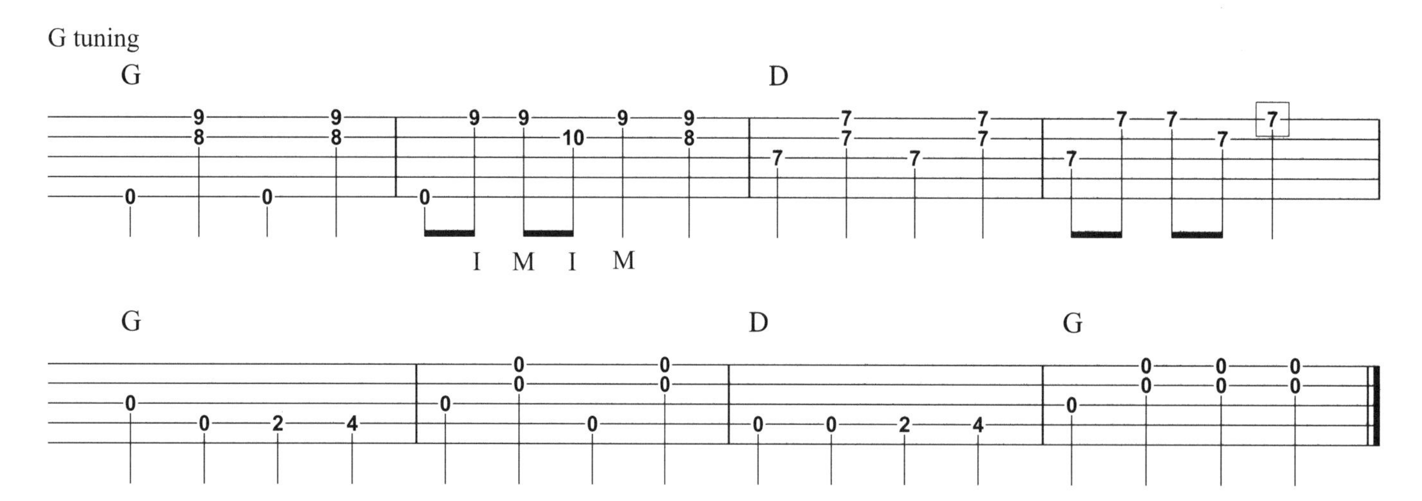

The next arrangement contains a classic element of the minstrel banjo style, i.e., a triplet figure followed by playing the fifth string open twice in succession. This note sequence is a distant relative of the Galax Lick via the later clawhammer banjo tradition. In any event, the song in question is *Get Away Old Maids Get Away,* as recorded by Chubby Parker; once again, elements of the parlor guitar accompaniment style are evident:

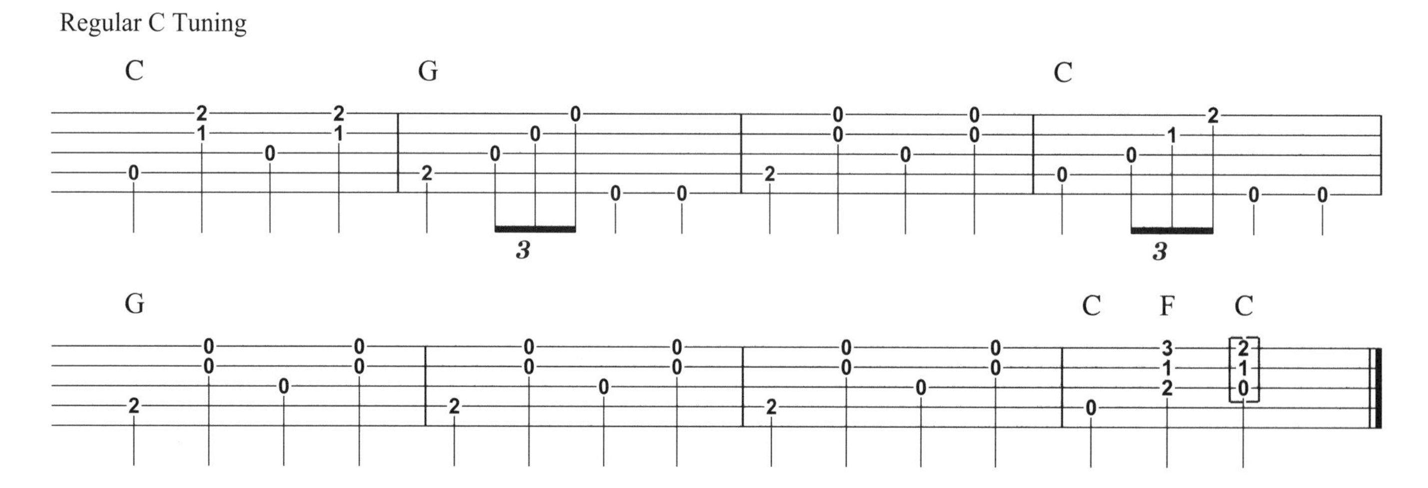

The backup to the song *Will the Weaver*, as recorded by Parker & Woodbright, is quite interesting because in that it uses a measure of 2/4, thus it is a crooked song:

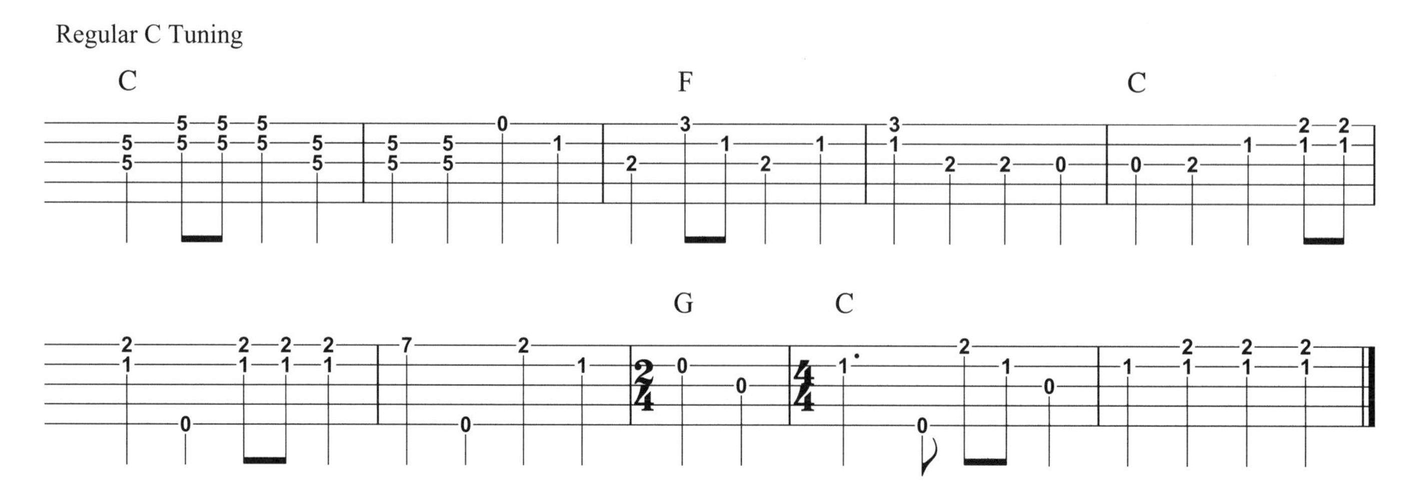

The C lick found in the penultimate measure is often played twice in a row during the song when the tonic chord is used:

Two Measure Lick:

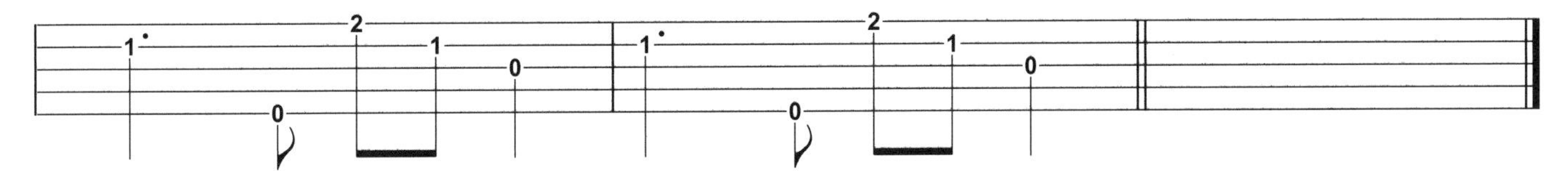

The backup to *My Home's Across the Blue Ridge Mountains,* as recorded by the Carolina Tar Heels, features use of the TIM forward roll. In measure 3 that roll accentuates the cross-string dissonance created by the minor to Major third interval, i.e., B flat to B (or for those more music theoretically-minded, an augmented second to the Major Third, i.e., A# to B natural):

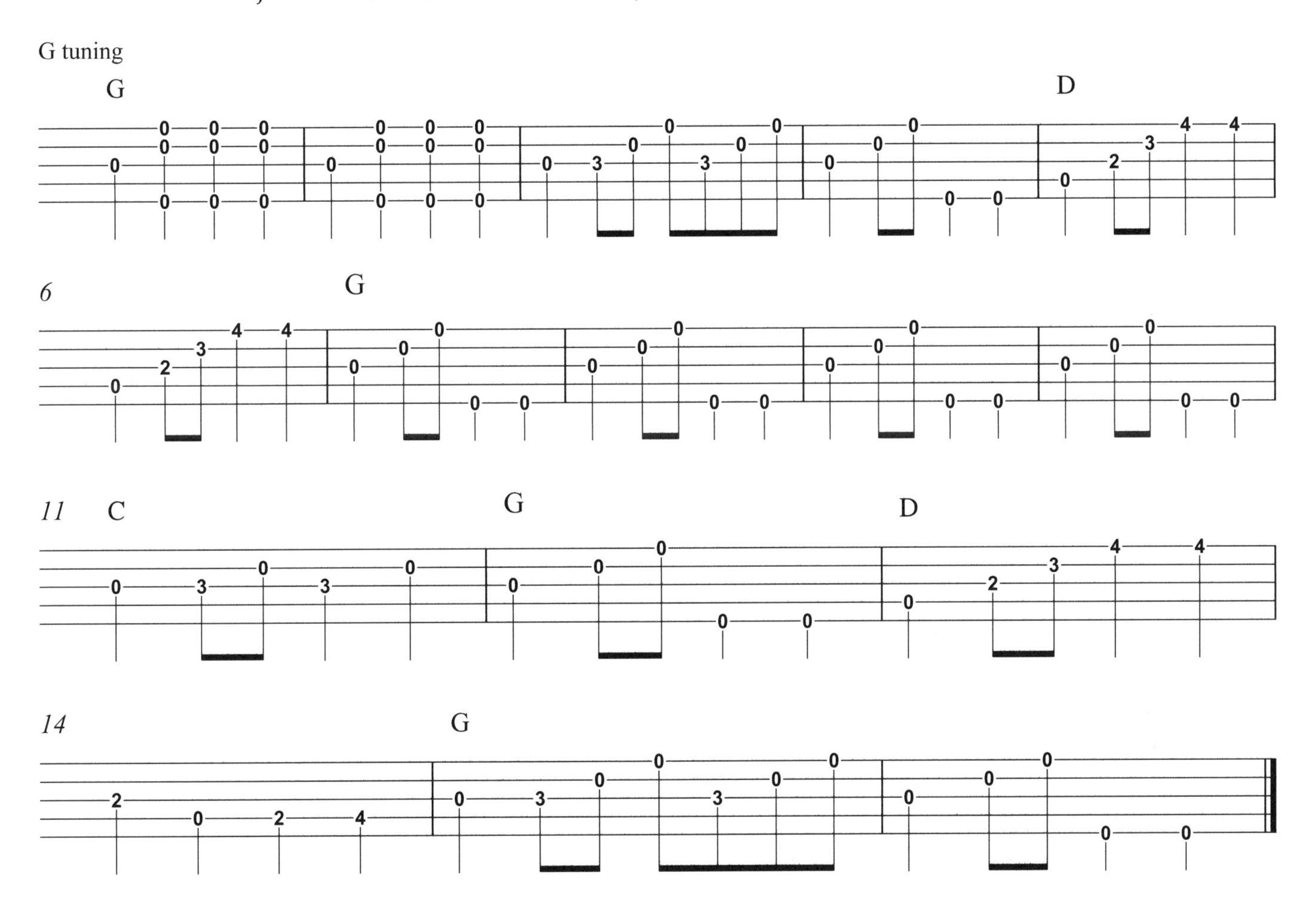

This backup also uses another roll that is roughly based on what would later become labeled as the forward-reverse bluegrass roll. This two-measure backup is used over the G tonic chord for one full chorus:

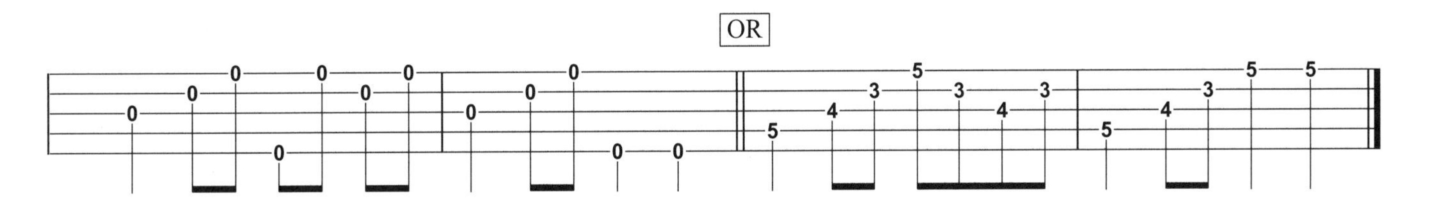

Let's now look at *Down on Penny's Farm*, as recorded by The Bentley Boys. The backup begins with an introduction by the banjo which features use of the TIM forward roll pattern in measures one and three:

G Tuning

Introduction:

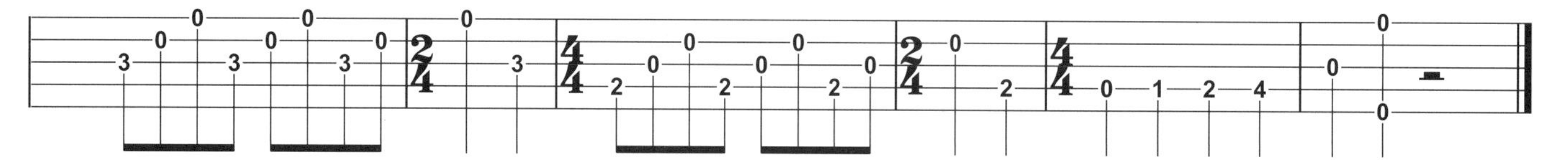

An "up the neck" solo is also featured, played out of the 12th and 7th positions, respectively:

G tuning XII

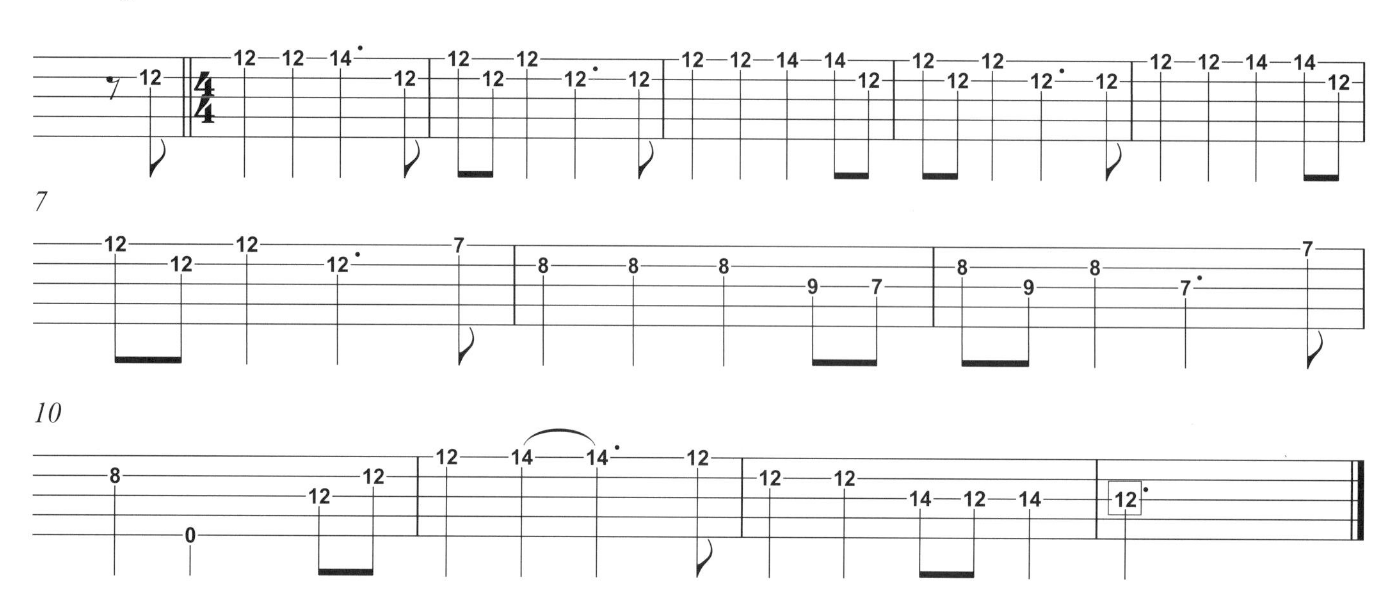

Next is the banjo solo for the popular song *Stack-O-Lee,* as recorded by the Fruit Jar Guzzlers:

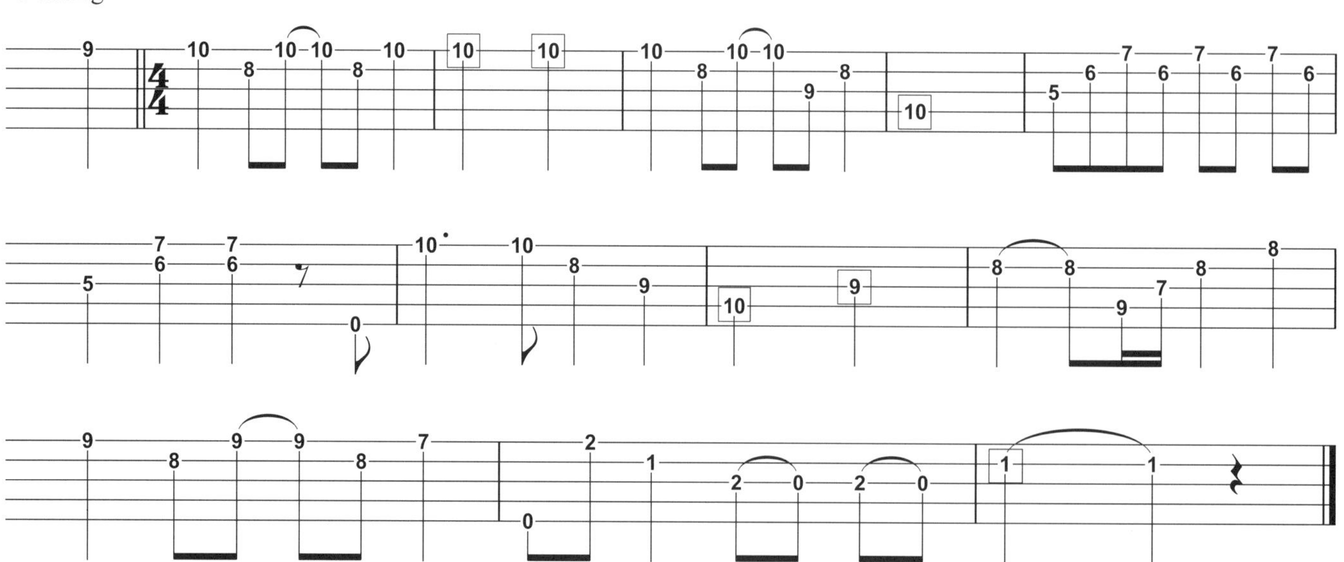

There are two main techniques used in this solo: the first is the use of a syncopated rhythmic figure in measures 1, 3 and 10; the second is the use of the TIMI arpeggio pattern over the IV chord, F, at measure 5, that is immediately followed by the same notes used in a pinch pattern (we saw that usage earlier, but in reverse order).

Let's now look at *A Pretty Girl's Love*, as recorded by Hendley-Whitter-Small. It uses 2-string index-lead style note sequences "up the neck" as well as some strummed chords and intervals (the latter in measure 10 is in the style of Bascom Lamar Lunsford, i.e., instead of playing those two notes alternately as was done in measure 1):

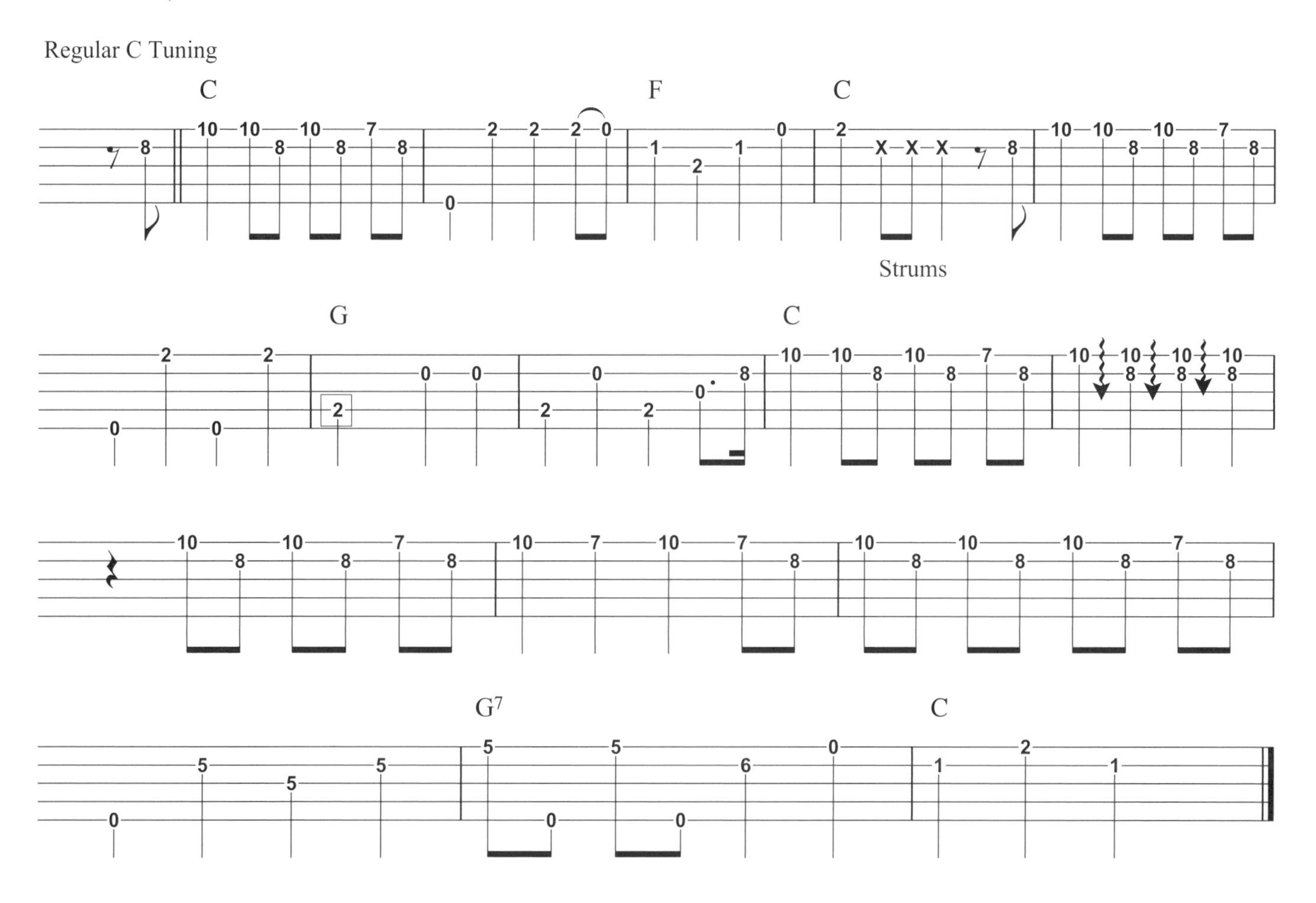

Posie Roach banjo player 1942, photo courtesy the Jim Mills Collection.

Speaking of Bascam Lamar Lunsford, let's look at his backup to the song, *Lulu Wall.* Note that his arrangement uses an unusual variation of the open G tuning (enharmonic with the elevated C tuning) in that the fifth string is tuned one whole note higher, i.e., from g to a:

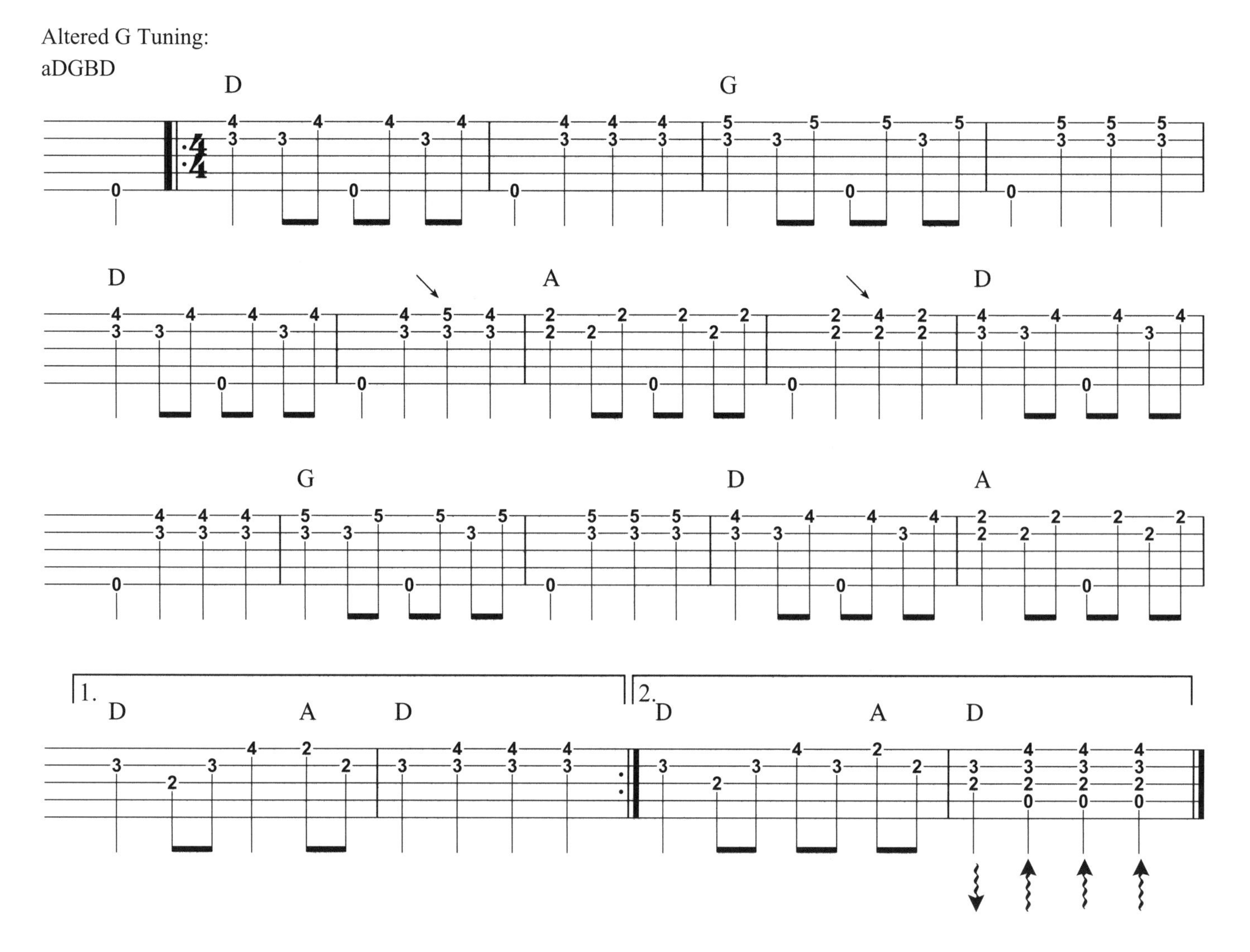

Lunsford uses several patterns in this backup. At the first ending he plays a forward-reverse-like roll pattern followed by a pinch pattern; at the second ending he varies the roll pattern, then he uses up-and-down strummed chords to end the song. Also, note the use of upper neighbor tones in measures 6 and 8 for harmonic interest.

Later on I will provide an arrangement of this backup in open D tuning; for the most part the only real difference will be the position of notes on the second string.

Here is a banjo solo by Flesher Hendley of a song called *Shuffle Feet Shuffle*, recorded on November 29, 1930 in Memphis, TN (here he was seconded once again by Henry Whitter and Marshall Small):

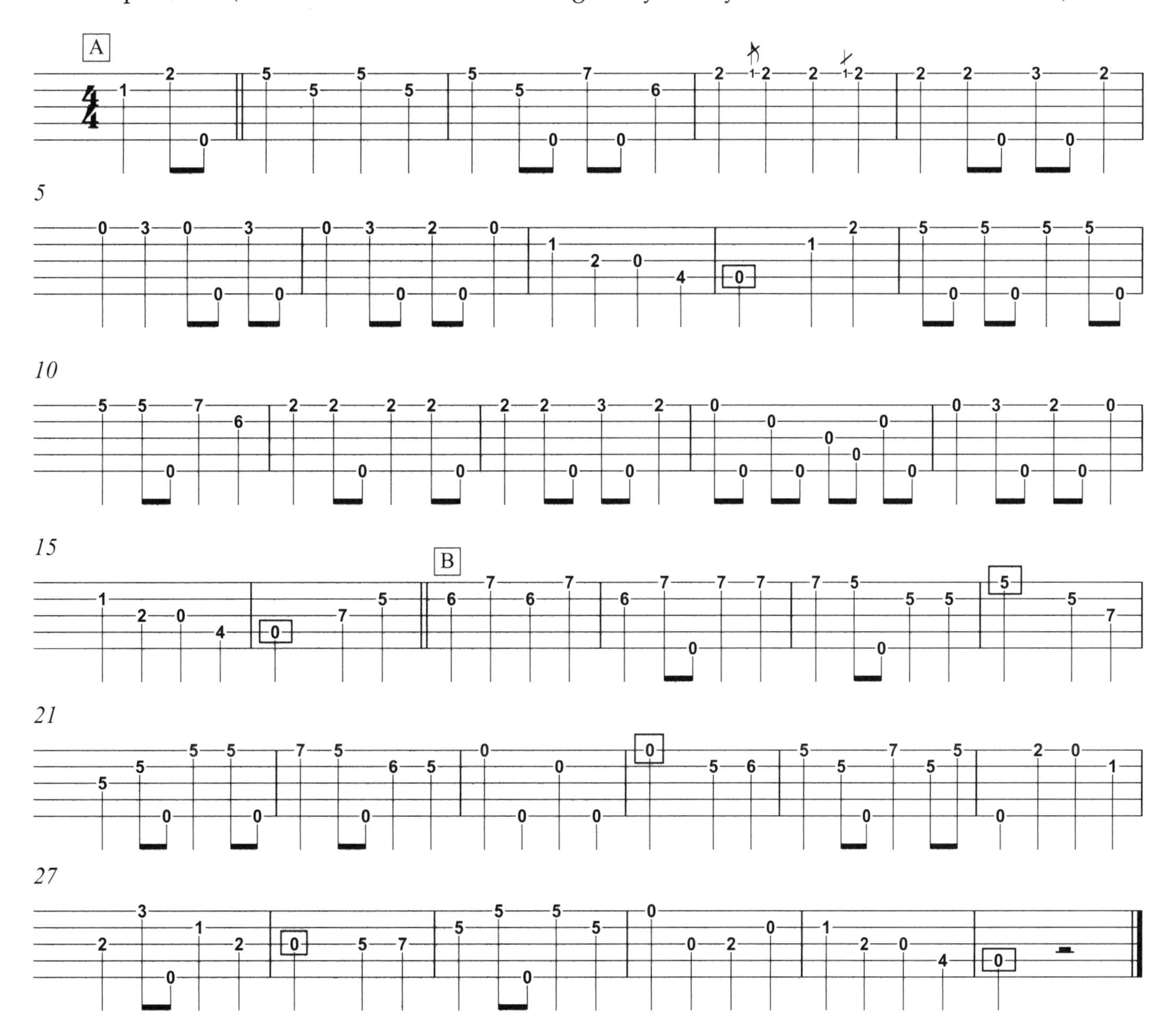

Uncle Dave Macon.

Most people probably associate raconteur Uncle Dave Macon with his appearances on The Grand Ole Opry radio broadcasts, as he was one of its original acts back in the day. However, he began his career some years earlier than that as a professional recording artist in 1924, when he was already in his mid-50s!

His songs often began with a banjo lick and a spoken introduction before he began to play his song or medley, as was often the case. Since he was primarily a solo act in his early career his banjo was more than just an instrument to provide a basic backup accompaniment to his vocals; he often included instrumental breaks in most of his songs, and the occasional solo as well.

As his instrumental breaks tend to include several idiomatic banjo techniques in any one song I have decided to present a number of transcriptions of such breaks by banjo tuning: Double C (gCGCD), open G tuning (gDGBD), open D tuning (f# D F# A D) and the open E tuning (g# E G# B E) and (the only difference in the latter two being that they are tuned one whole step apart).

Songs using Double C Tuning.

Let's begin by looking at a clawhammer arrangement for the song *I'm Going to Leave You Love*. The primary feature of this bridge riff is use of a 2-4 slide on the second string; Macon heavily accents the initial note and then slowly drags it to the fourth fret. He could have used a 0-2 open string hammer-on on the first string but he wouldn't have been able to imitate his vocal slide using that technique.

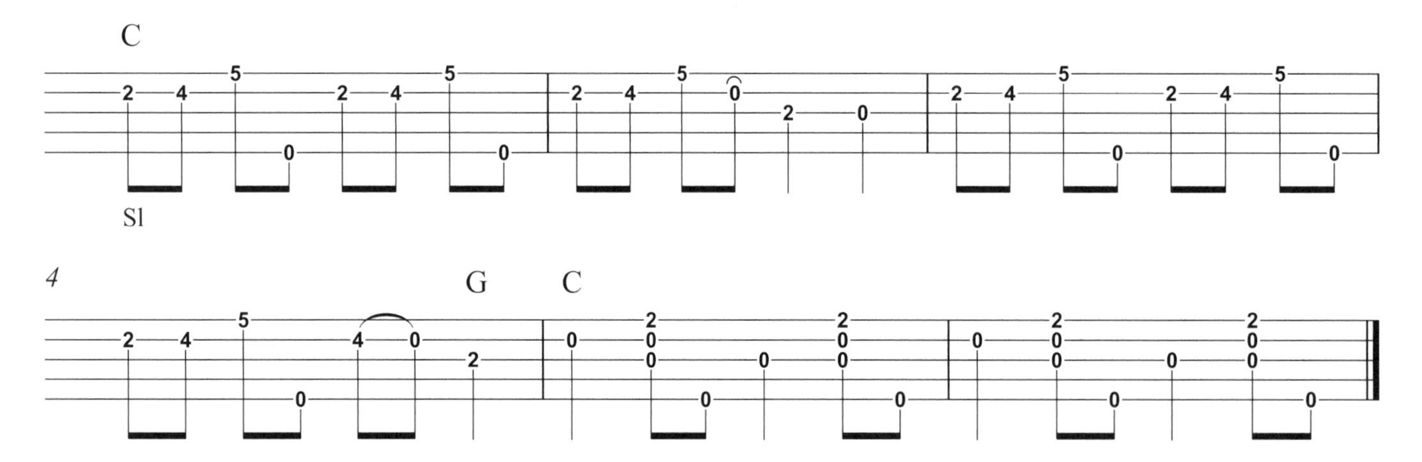

Also make note of the use of the open string pull off technique used in measure two.

Songs using Open G Tuning.

The instrumental break used in the song *The Old Log Cabin in the Lane* is pretty straight forward using thumb lead technique:

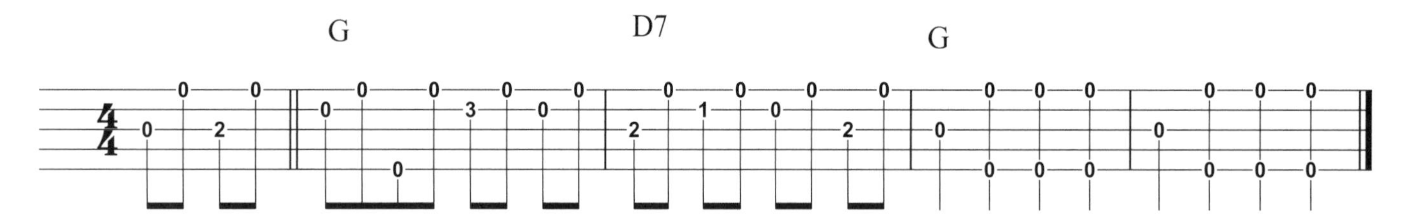

Macon also used this same break, with the exception of using triplet figures in the first measure, in the song *Jonah and the Whale.*

The solo break for the song *Down by the River* is based on thumb lead but also incorporates parlor guitar backup patterns for the triplet figure in the first measure and variations on this figure in measures four and five:

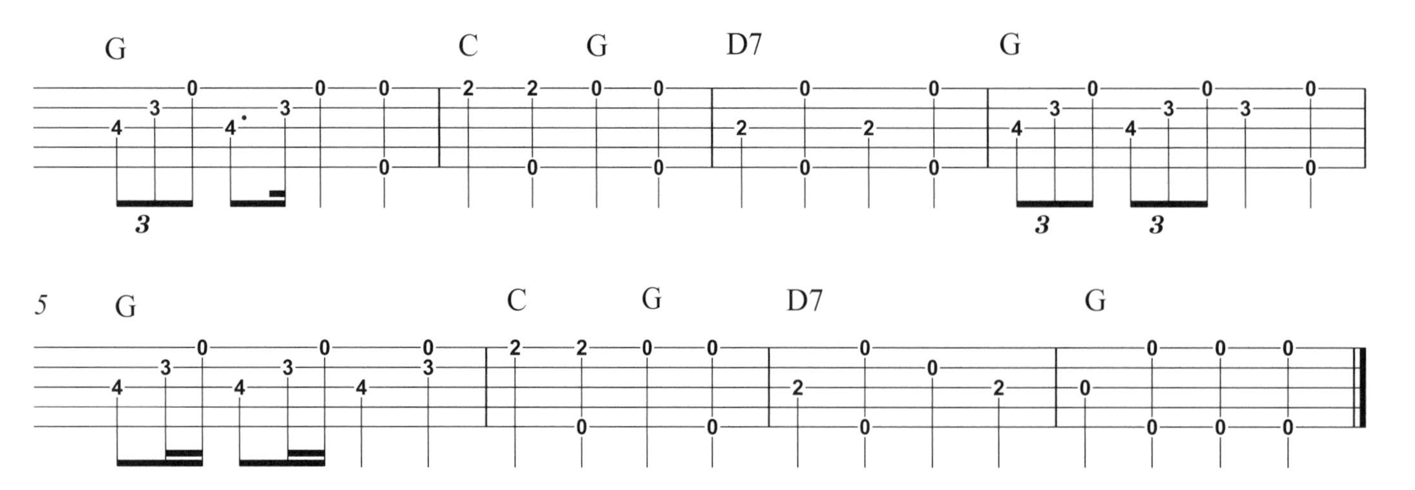

Open D and Open E Tunings.
About half of the songs that Macon recorded during the period 1924-25 are in either open D or open E tunings (open D and open E tunings appear identical in banjo tablature except, perhaps, for the fifth string note). Before I present those examples I should mention the fact that the difference in the intervallic relationships between the open G tuning and open D or E tunings results in the use of the basic thumb lead pattern vs. a parlor guitar arpeggio-like roll respectively.

The basic root position triad in open G tuning is found on the open third, second, and first strings respectively, with the octave note positioned on the fifth string; in open D or E tuning the root is found on the fourth string, the third on the third string, the fifth on the second string and the octave note on the first string; the fifth string is thus tuned to the third of the chord in open E tuning or to the third or fifth in open D tuning (due to the fact that if you attempted to tune the fifth string higher than an A note it will usually break). Here is an example comparing the two patterns resulting simply from the difference in tuning:

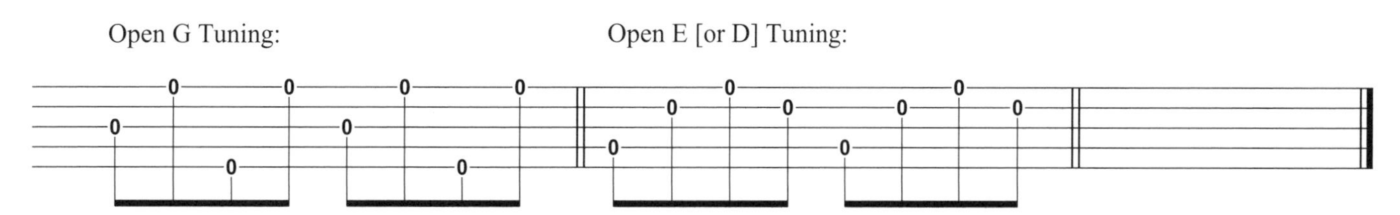

Songs using Open D Tuning.
Keeping this in mind, and how it affects the appearance of notes in the banjo tablature, let's look at the backup for the song *Just from Tennessee*:

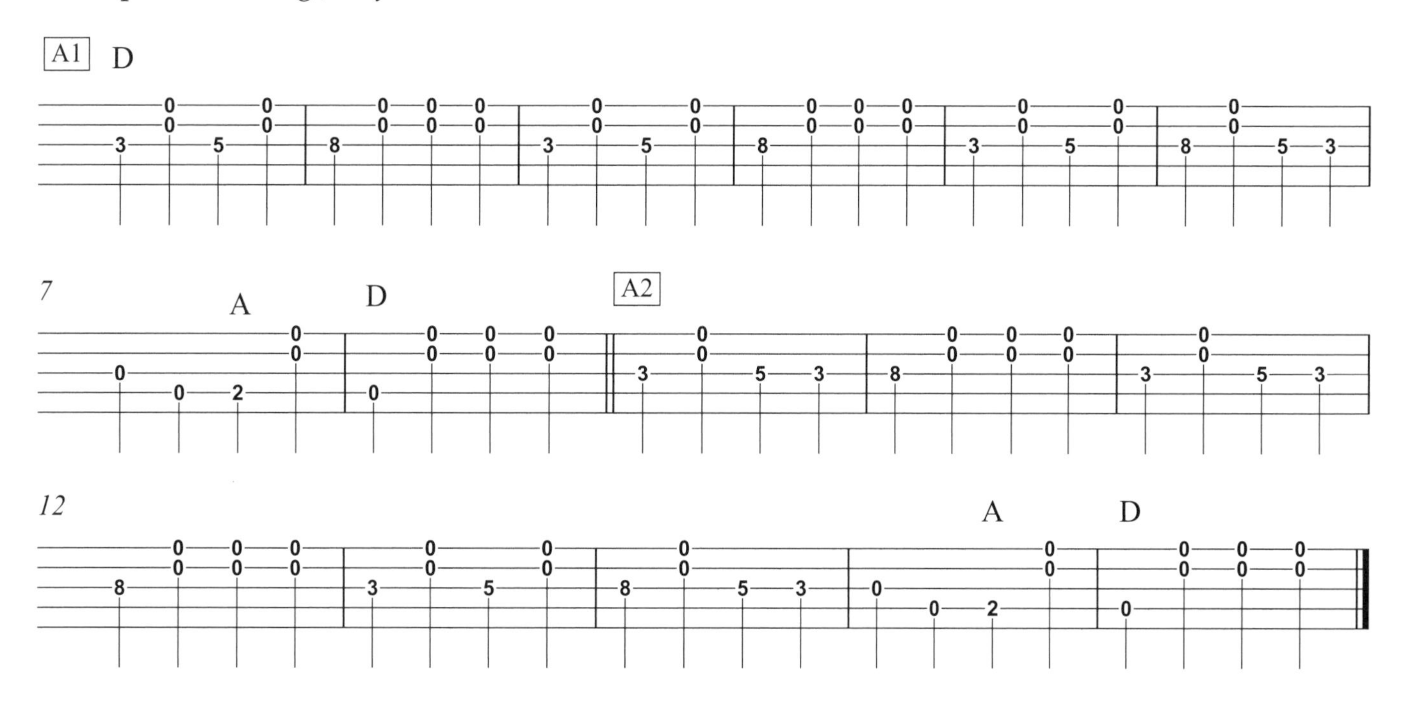

As you can see, the break uses the basic parlor guitar accompaniment technique.

The next two songs in open D tuning utilize the basic thumb-lead technique. The first song is *Station will be Changed after a While*:

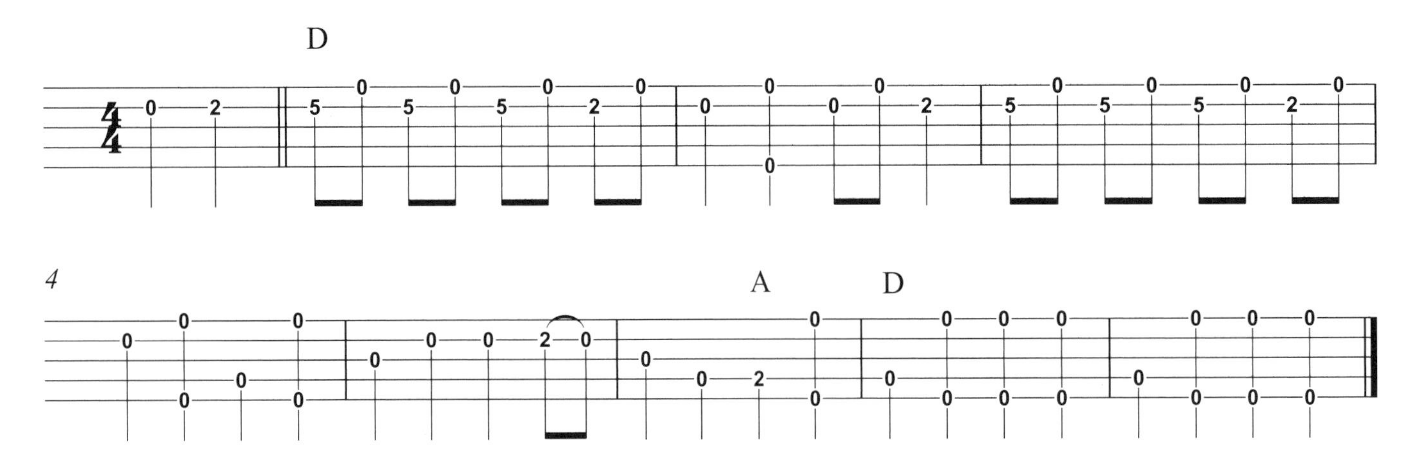

Note that the break for the song *Run, N_____r, Run* (aka *The Patroller Song*) incorporates some open string pull offs in measures one and three:

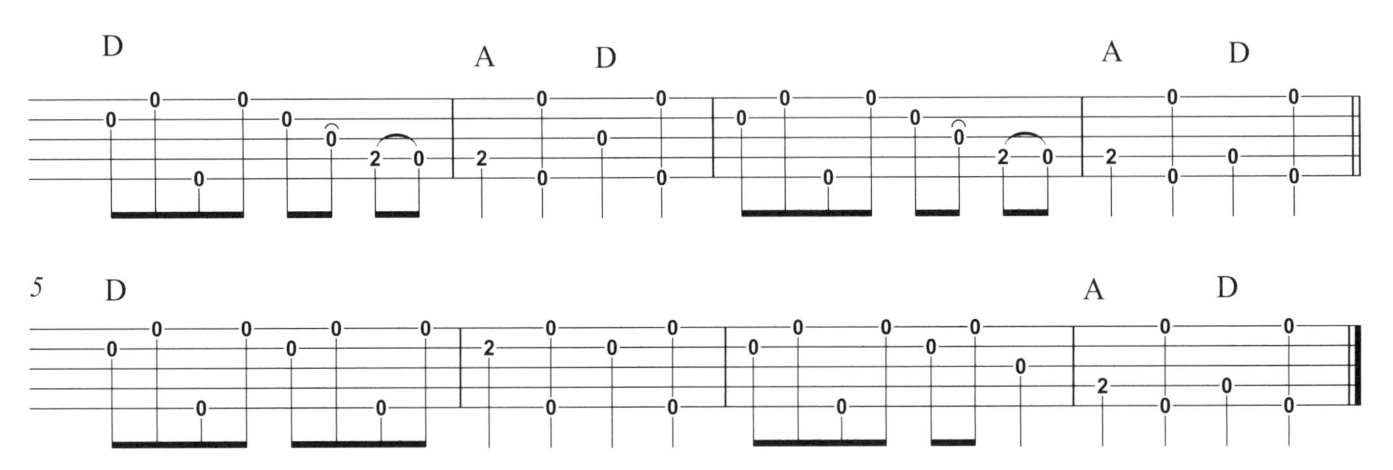

Songs using Open E Tuning.

The first song in open E tuning, *Hill-Billie Blues*, once again relies upon basic parlor guitar accompaniment technique for the backup:

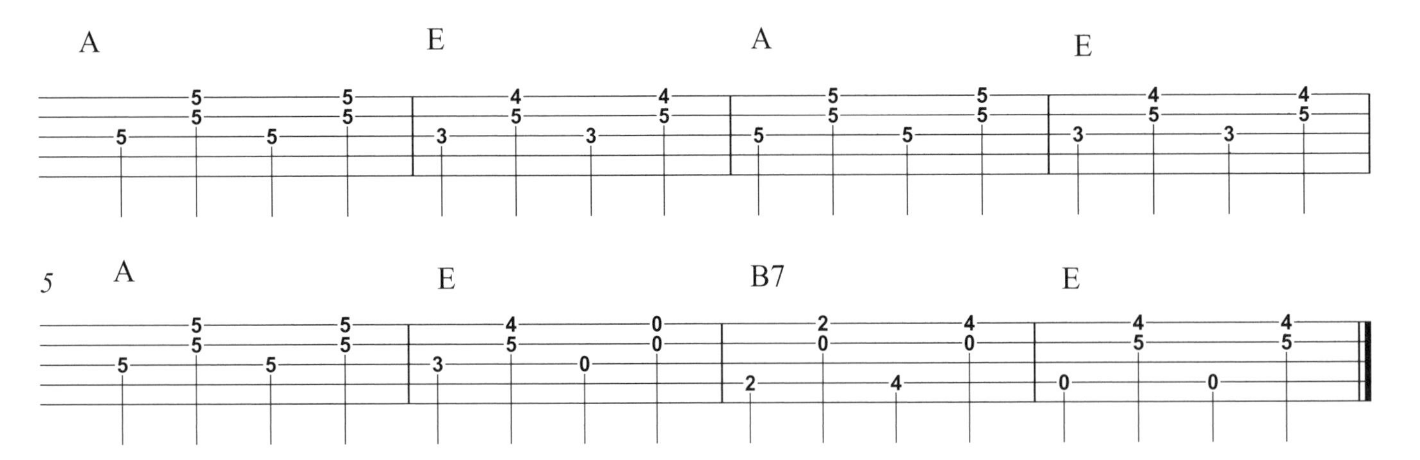

In the song *From Jerusalem to Jericho* the basic block chord backup pattern is broken up into an arpeggio-like roll in measures one and three:

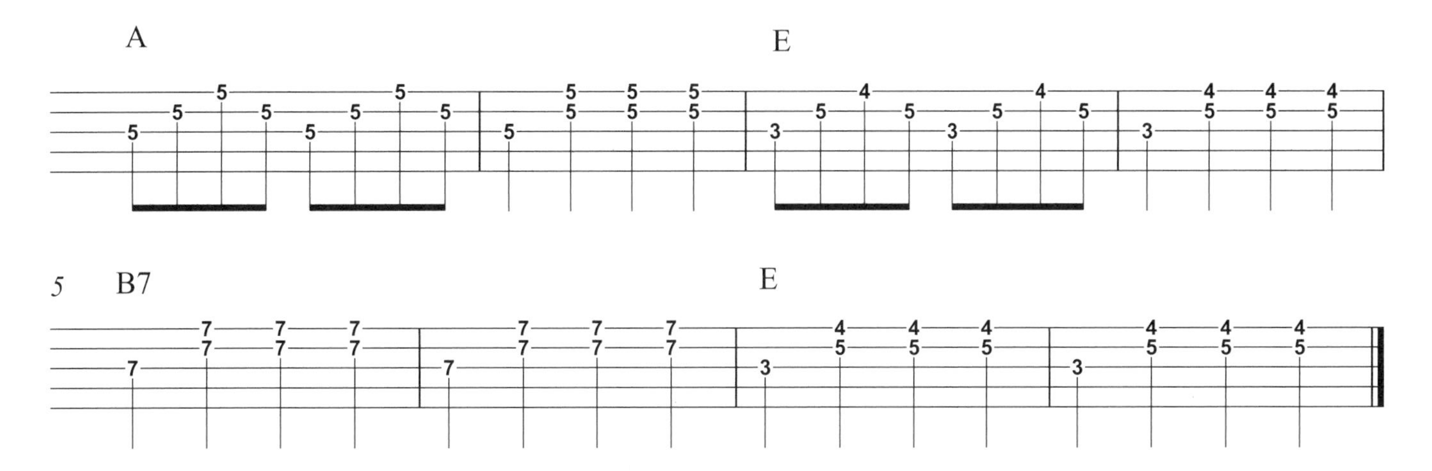

Similarly, in the song *Old Maid's Last Hope*, the block chord pattern is broken up into a reverse roll pattern [3-3-2] in measures two and five:

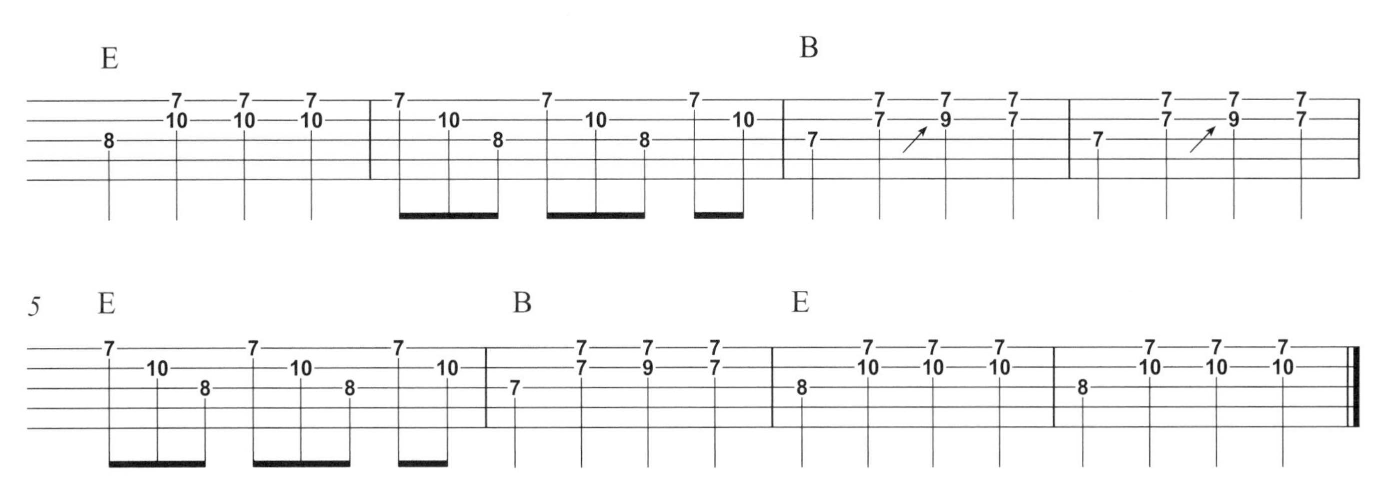

In the break to the song *All Go Hungry Hash House* the initial measure uses thumb-lead while the remaining measures in the break uses parlor guitar-style backup:

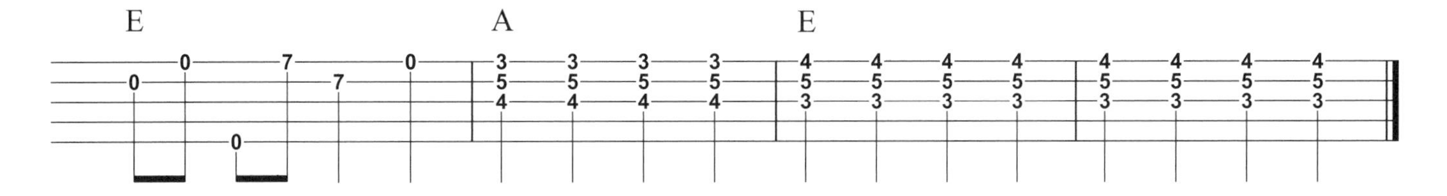

Thumb-lead is the principle technique used for the solo *I Tickled Nancy*; however, a roll pattern opens the break and double stops are also used in measures five and six:

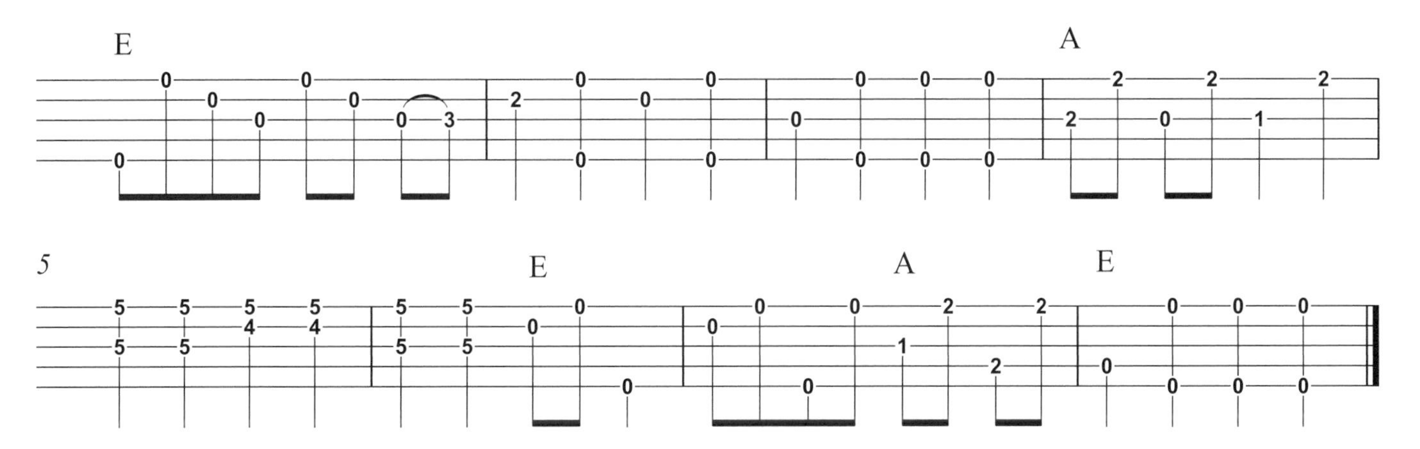

Triplet figures open up the instrumental break to the song *All I've Gots Gone*:

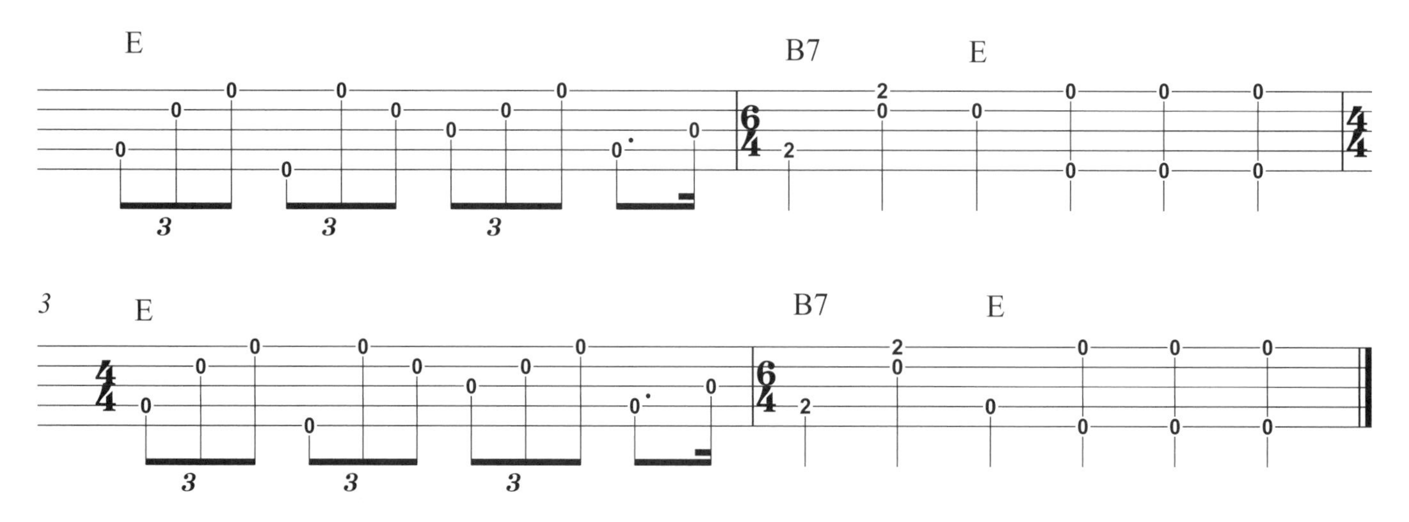

As you can see here in the two measures in 6/4 time Macon used the open E tuning double stop pattern as well as the thumb-lead pattern in tandem.

The following song, *Sugar in the Gourd*, uses all of the techniques that I have just been outlining:

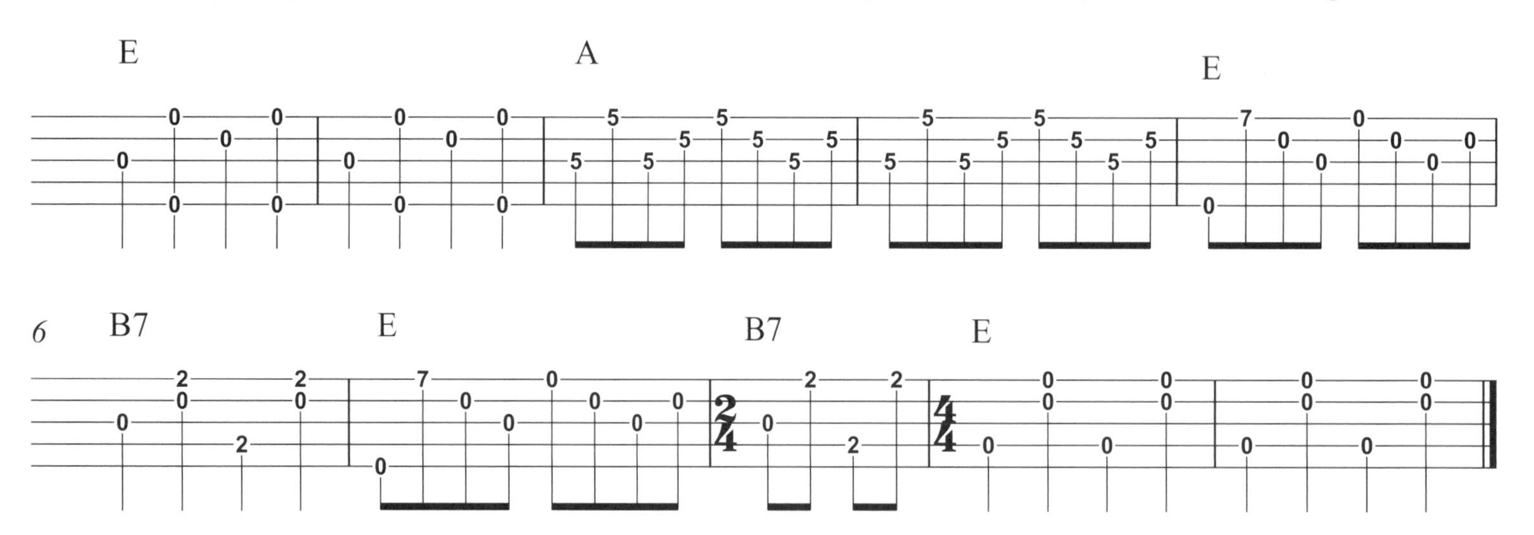

Let's close this section on Uncle Dave Macon with his solo in open E tuning for the song *Watermelon Smilin' on a Vine*:

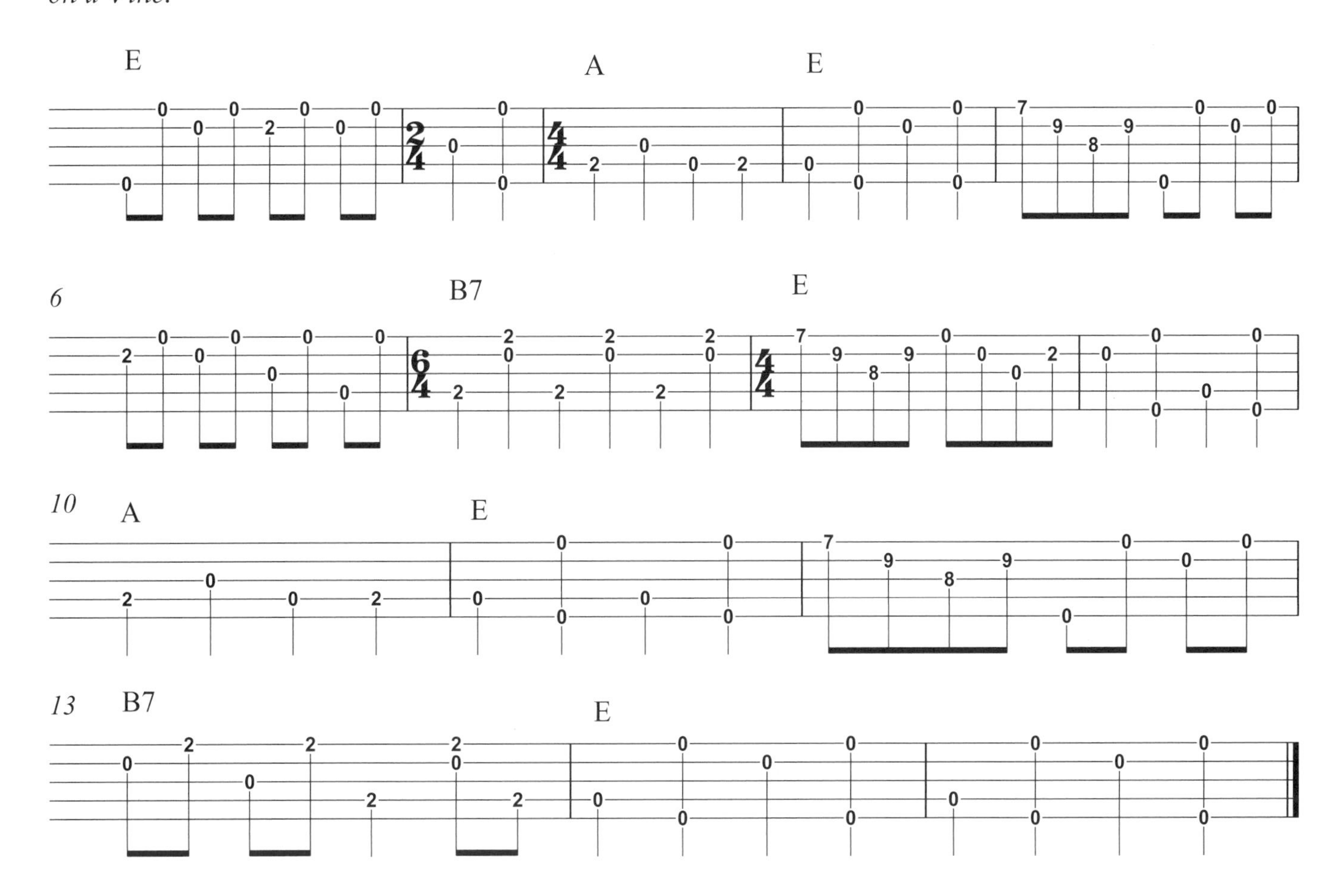

As you can see from these short extracts Macon used any number of techniques in any one instrumental break or solo instead of the standard practice of repeated backup patterns; he also often doubled the melody as he sang, often utilizing what he would use for his instrumental break.

Photo courtesy the Jim Mills Collection.

This would be a good place for me to show you the backup in open D tuning that I promised you earlier of Bascam Lamar Lunsford's song *Lulu Wall*:

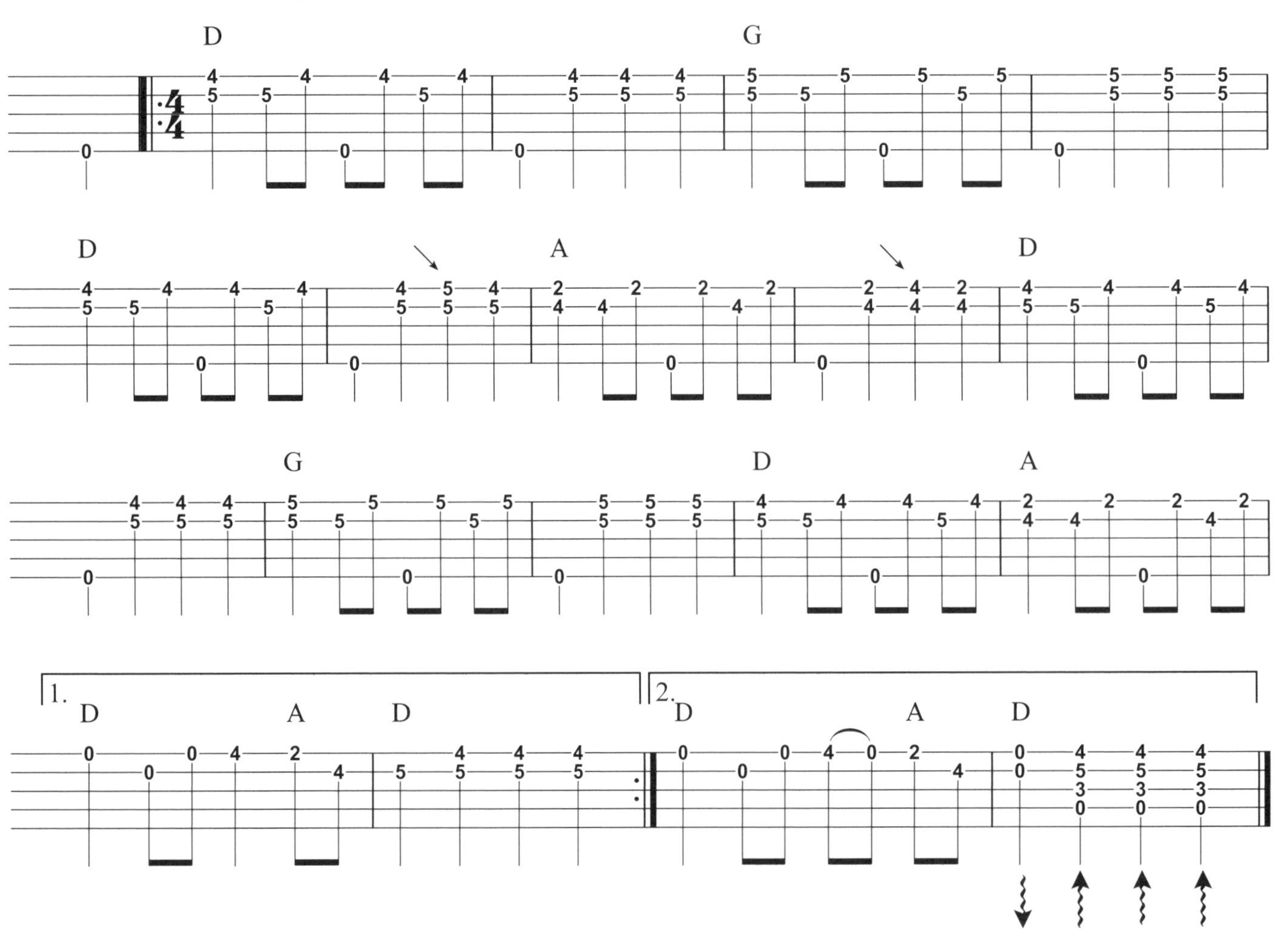

Syncopated Banjo Solos.
Let's look at a highly syncopated and rhythmically intricate backup used in the song *John Hardy*, as recorded by Ernest V. Stoneman on July 9, 1928 (the banjo player was Earl Sweet):

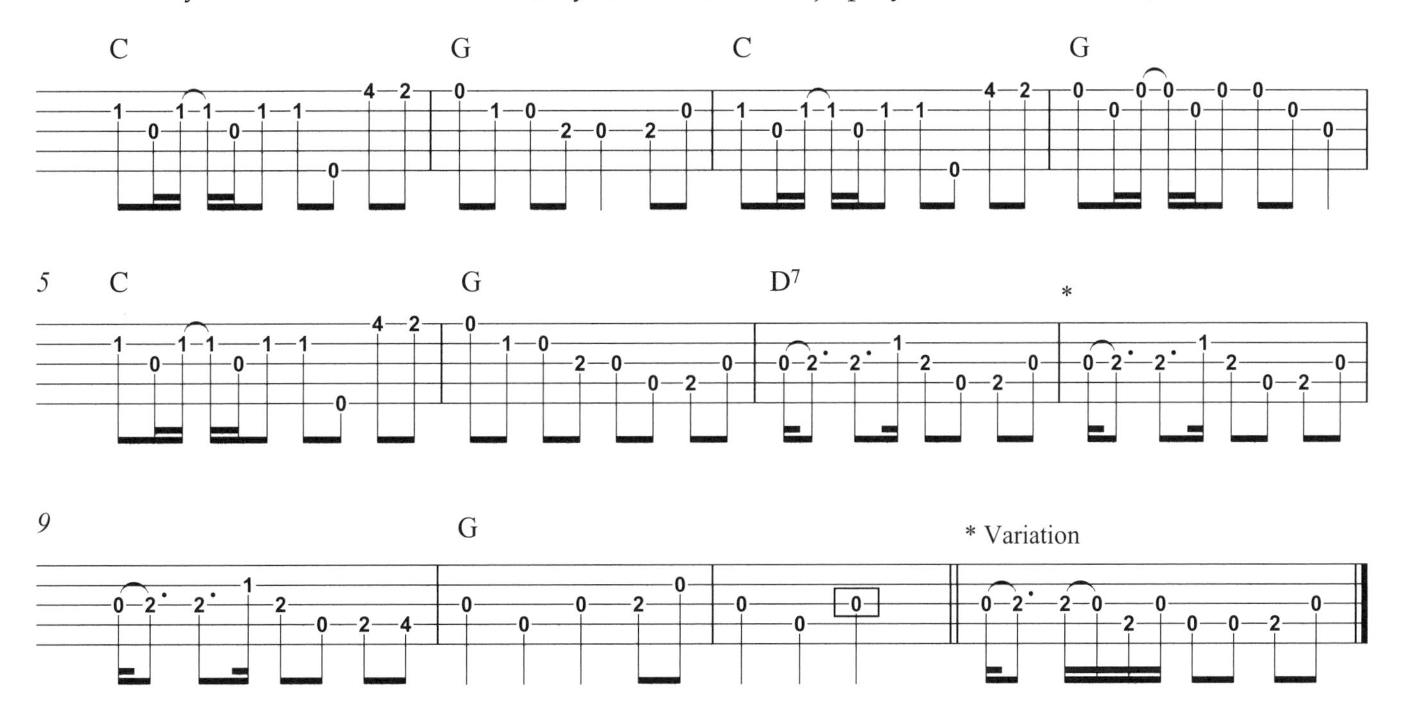

As you have seen so far, many of the banjo backup techniques used in string band recordings were based on parlor guitar finger picking techniques, basic thumb-lead style backup patterns, or a combination of thumb-lead style and finger picking. When index-lead patterns are reversed, or played in a closed position, the thumb-lead style often results. There are also lots of rhythmically varied arpeggio patterns, based on TIM and TIMI, used throughout those recordings.

Frank Jenkins.
One banjoist whose name is often associated with the development of a syncopated bluegrass banjo-like roll pattern during the 1920's string band period was North Carolinian Frank Jenkins, who was adept in the classic three-finger banjo style. He recorded a number of "sides" with DaCosta Woltz's Southern Broadcasters in May 1927 (both he and Woltz played banjo on most of those recordings). It was during those sessions that Jenkins also recorded two banjo solos, *Baptist Shout* and *Home, Sweet Home*. A couple of years later, during late summer 1929, he played fiddle on a number of recordings, first with Oscar Jenkin's Mountaineers, then with his own ensemble, Frank Jenkin's Pilot Moutaineers. Oscar was Frank's then 19-year old son, who played thumb-lead banjo for the latter two sessions. I have previously presented examples of the backups for some of the songs which they recorded.

Earlier I discussed some rhythmic backup licks that were used in the song *Curly Headed Woman* that was also recorded around the same time as this song. You will find evidence of their usage in Section A of this transcription of *Baptist Shout*:

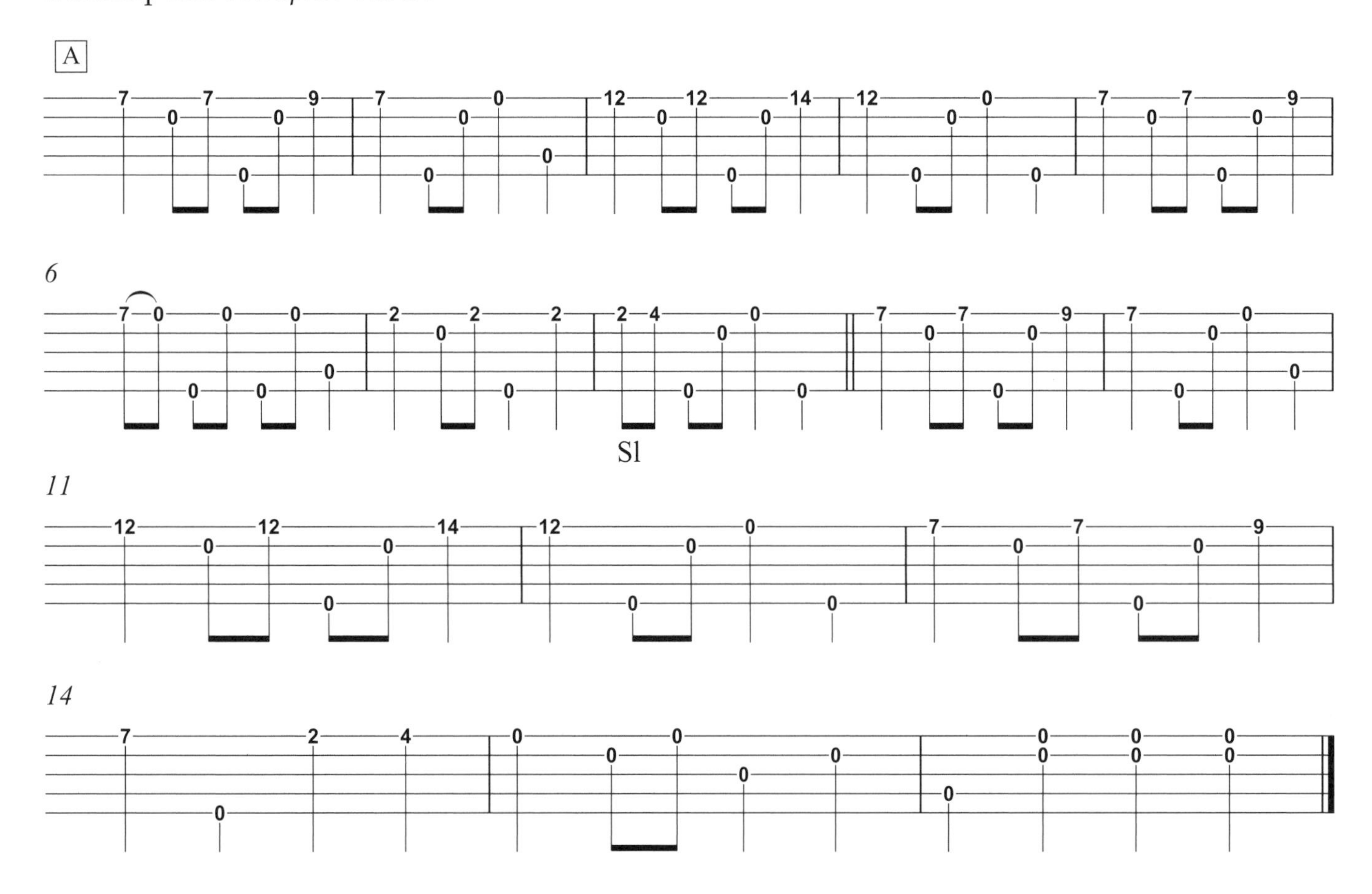

The pattern that Frank Jenkins used in Section A of *Baptist Shout* was loosely based on the following syncopated rhythmic pattern -- dotted quarter note-dotted quarter note-quarter note -- a syncopated pattern that later became one of the commonly used forward roll patterns used in Scruggs-style bluegrass banjo:

Section B of *Baptist Shout* features a rolling arpeggio figure in measures 1-2 and 5-6 that we have seen used in numerous examples presented throughout this book:

The thumb-index two-finger style was the earliest way that country blues guitar was played (e.g., Huddie "Lead Belly" Ledbetter [b. 1888] and Charlie Patton [b. 1891]); however, some blues guitar players soon began to incorporate the occasional use of the middle finger on the first string (e.g., "Mississippi" John Hurt [b. 1893]). At some point in time this middle finger usage was transferred over to the banjo creating an additional drone string on the second string that, in turn, opened up the possibility for new thumb-lead roll variations:

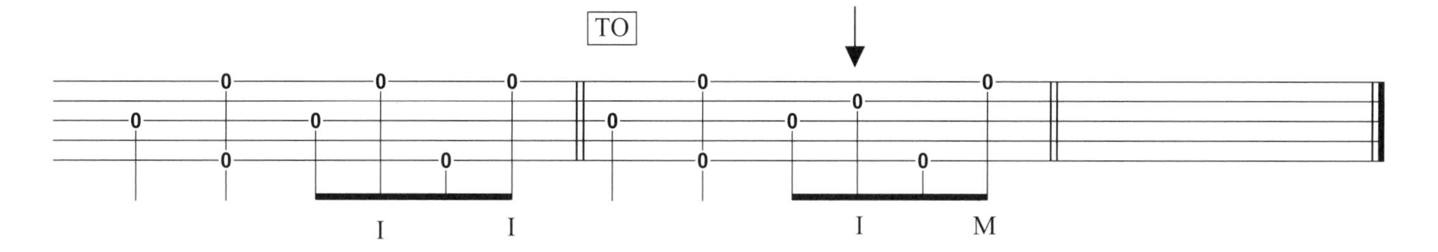

Bridge Riffs and Hooks. Occasionally, the banjoist only played a short lick acting as a bridge signaling a return back to the verse or to an instrumental break, as in the song *Gone to Germany* recorded by Cannon's Jug Stompers:

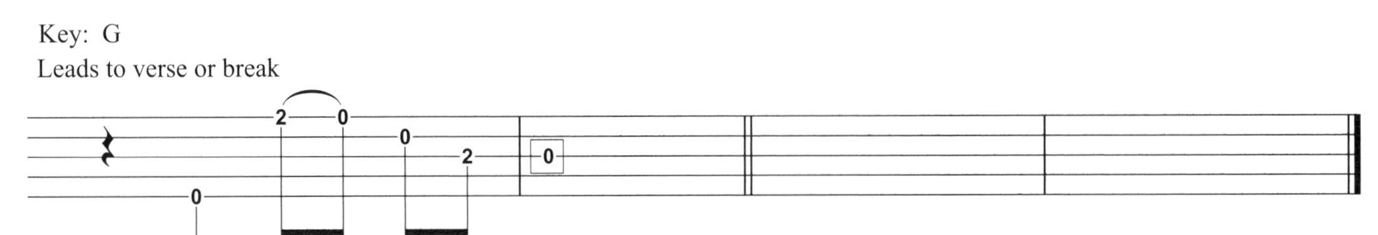

Here is a "hook" over the G tonic chord that is based on a guitar lick which includes a chromatic passing tone, as well as an augmented second to Major Third dissonant interval:

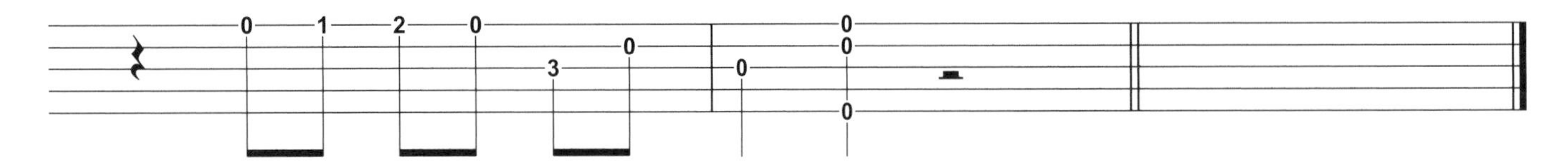

Next is yet another hook for the fiddle tune *Sally Goodin*, discussed earlier:

Key: G
G Tuning

Repeated Hook

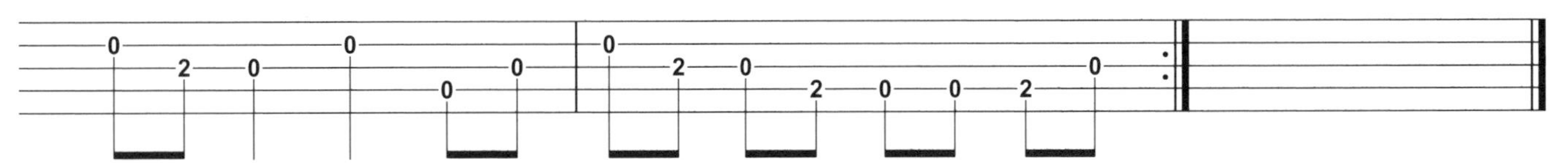

Here is a similar instance where Uncle Dave Macon used a short instrumental bridge to return to the verse for the song *All In Down and Out*:

Regular C Tuning

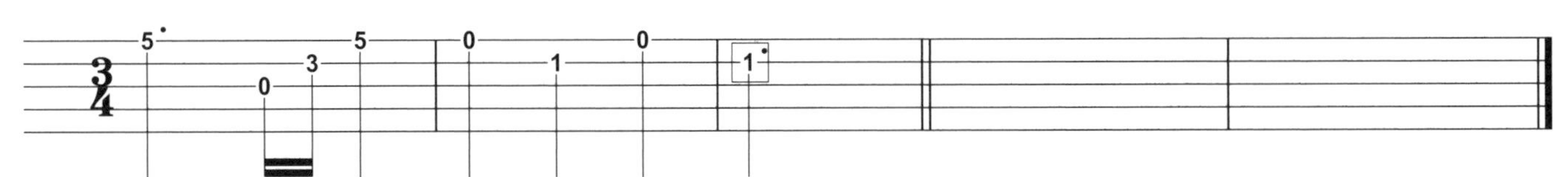

Next is the instrumental bridge used in the song that I presented earlier, *Get Away Old Maids Get Away* as recorded by Chubby Parker:

Regular C Tuning

Instrumental Bridge:

SONGS IN TRIPLE METER (3/4)

The following pinch pattern is the one used most frequently in triple meter (¾) songs:

Triple Meter Pinch Pattern

Here are some of the songs in triple meter from the string band genre which used this technique, among countless others:

Don't You Remember the Time
Freeny's Barn Dance Band

The Eastbound Train
Ernest V. Stoneman and His Dixie Mountaineers

George Collins
Roy Harvey and the North Carolina Ramblers

I Know My Name is There
Da Costa Woltz's Southern Broadcasters

Lost Love Blues
Dock Boggs

My Mother and My Sweetheart
Ernest V. Stoneman and His Dixie Mountaineers

Nobody's Darling
North Carolina Ridge Runners

The Prisoner's Lament
Ernest V. Stoneman and His Dixie Mountaineers

There'll Come A Time
Ernest V. Stoneman and His Dixie Mountaineers

Wednesday Night Waltz
Leake County Revelers

The strumming technique that I discussed earlier can also be used in songs in triple meter, i.e., 3/4. The backup for the song, *The Rose With a Broken Stem* as recorded by the North Carolina Cooper Boys, is based on the following pattern:

Backup Rhythm:

In the next example, the song *George Collins* as recorded by Roy Harvey and the North Carolina Ramblers, the banjoist played 16th notes on the weak beats. Here is that rhythmic pattern:

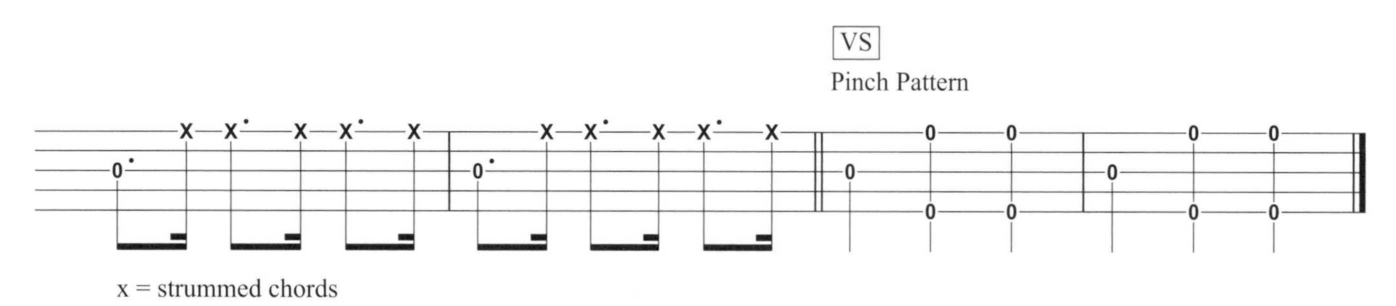

Next is a basic backup used by Fisher Hendley in his recording of the song *Blind Child's Prayer* that uses a basic pinch pattern or a 2-beat thumb-lead roll followed by a broken pinch on beat 3 to complete the pattern:

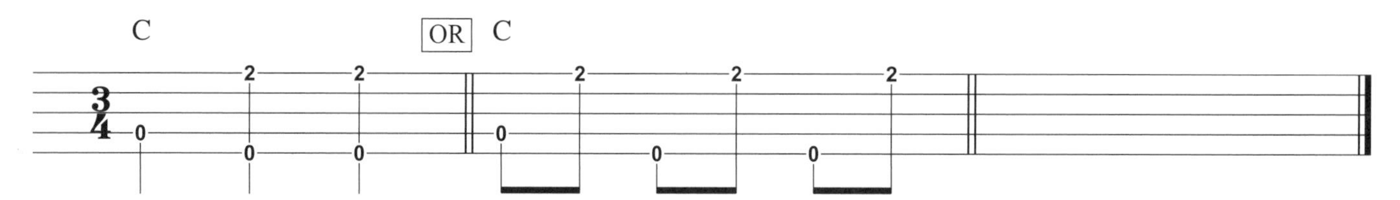

The banjo backup for the song *Got Drunk and Got Married*, which I covered earlier, uses this guitar-style pinch pattern:

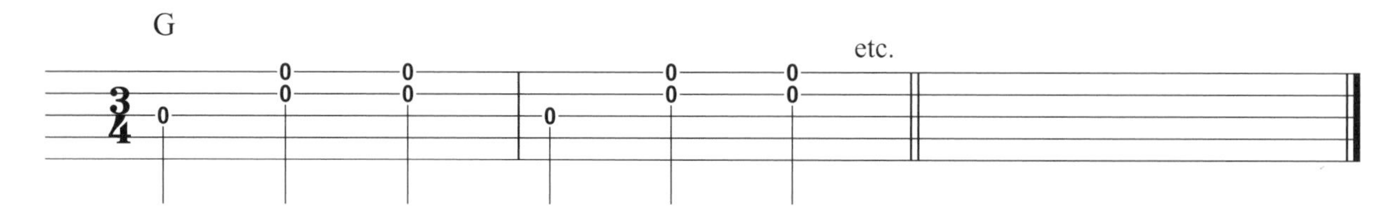

At the coda to this song the following note sequence is used:

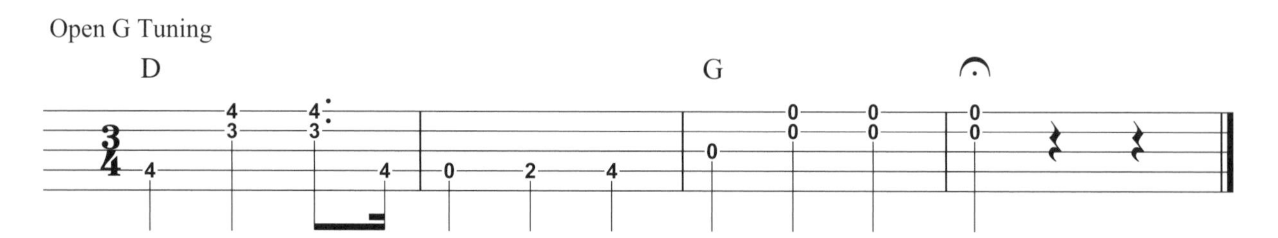

Let's now look at the song *Jack of Diamonds* as recorded by Ben Jarrell, father of the famous old-time fiddler Tommy Jarrell. His backup is fairly close to what the first generation of bluegrass banjoists might have used for songs in triple meter; in particular, make note of the *double double* note sequence used on beats 2 and 3:

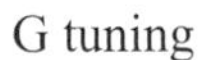

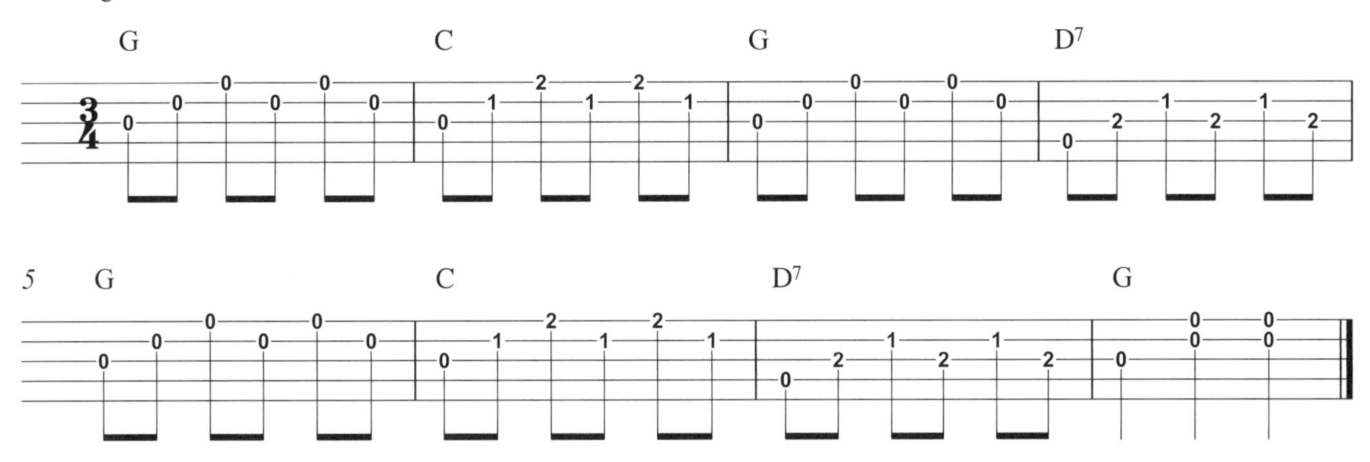

An "up the neck" backup is also featured:

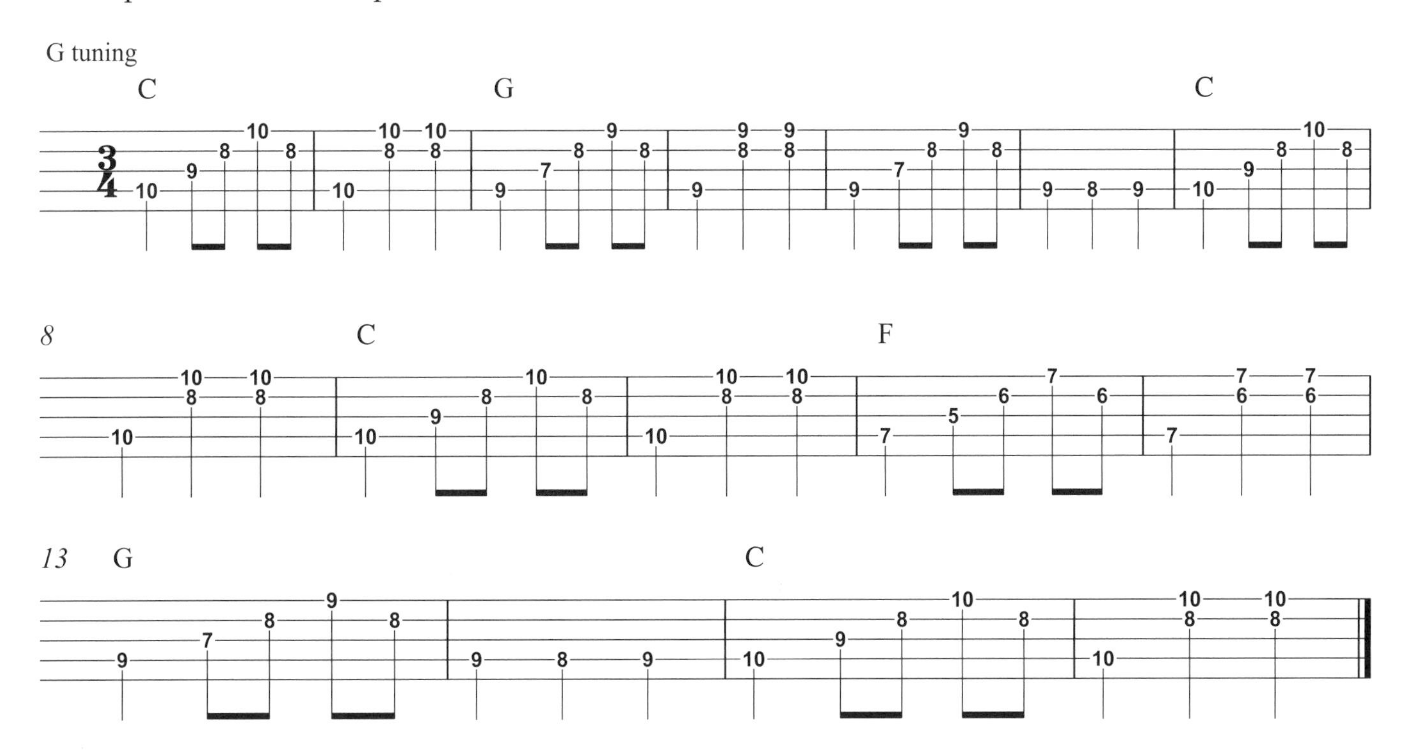

The backup for the song *In the Pines*, as recorded on April 17, 1926 by "Dock" Coble Walsh, features three items of interest. The first is use of the forward-reverse roll pattern in measures 6-7, followed by a TIM forward roll in the next measure:

G Tuning

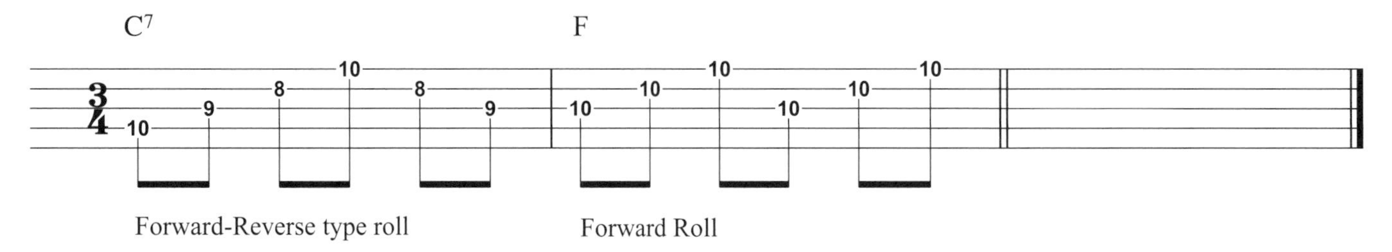

The following note sequence is usually played by Walsh over the tonic F chord when he plays it for two measures in succession, e.g., at measures 1-2 and 7-8:

G Tuning

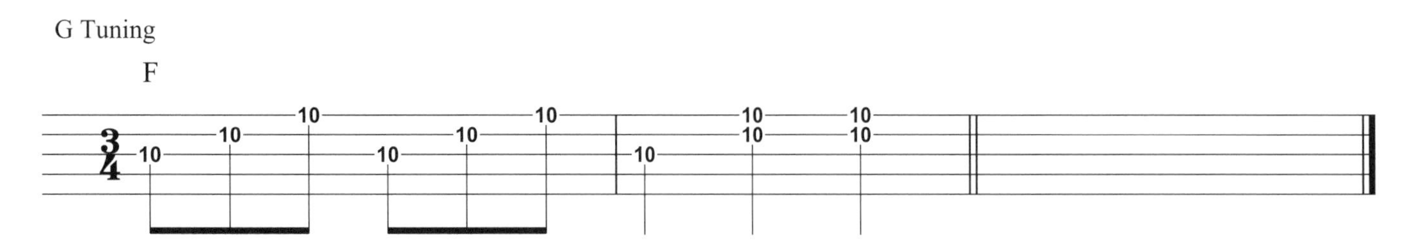

During another 8-measure chorus he uses the following "up the neck" syncopated roll over the chords:

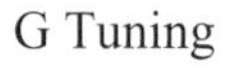

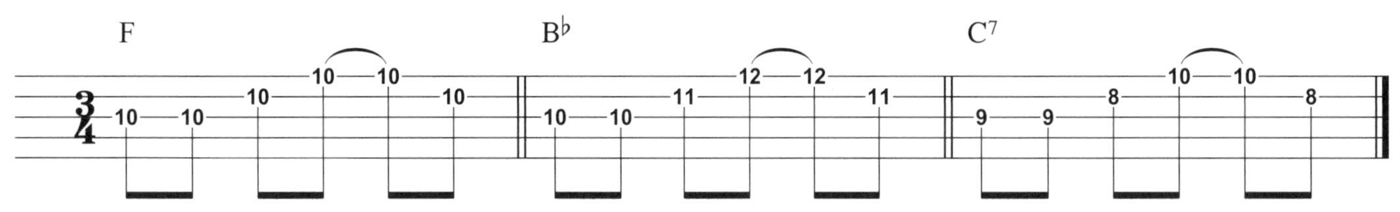

Finally, here is a complete composite of Walsh's basic 8-measure backup:

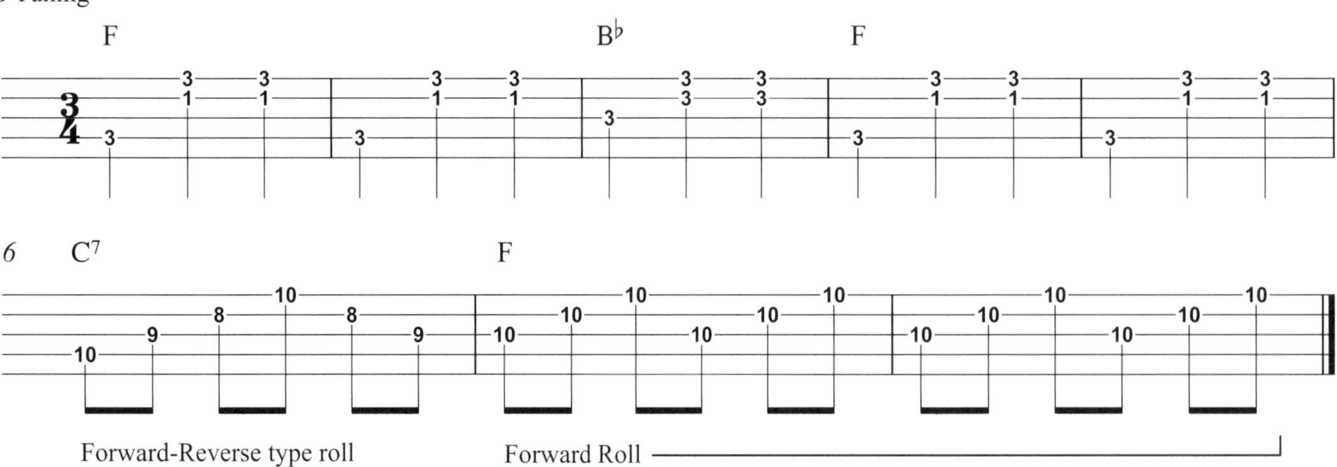

The last backup to look at in triple meter is for the song *The Dixie Cowboy*, as recorded by Taylor's Kentucky Boys in April 1927. The song was recorded in A Major but I am playing it out of the key of G (using elevated tuning, i.e., C to D) tuning up the fifth string one whole step to A, and then using a capo at the second fret. Note the use of the triplet figures and the concluding G octave notes in the penultimate measure.

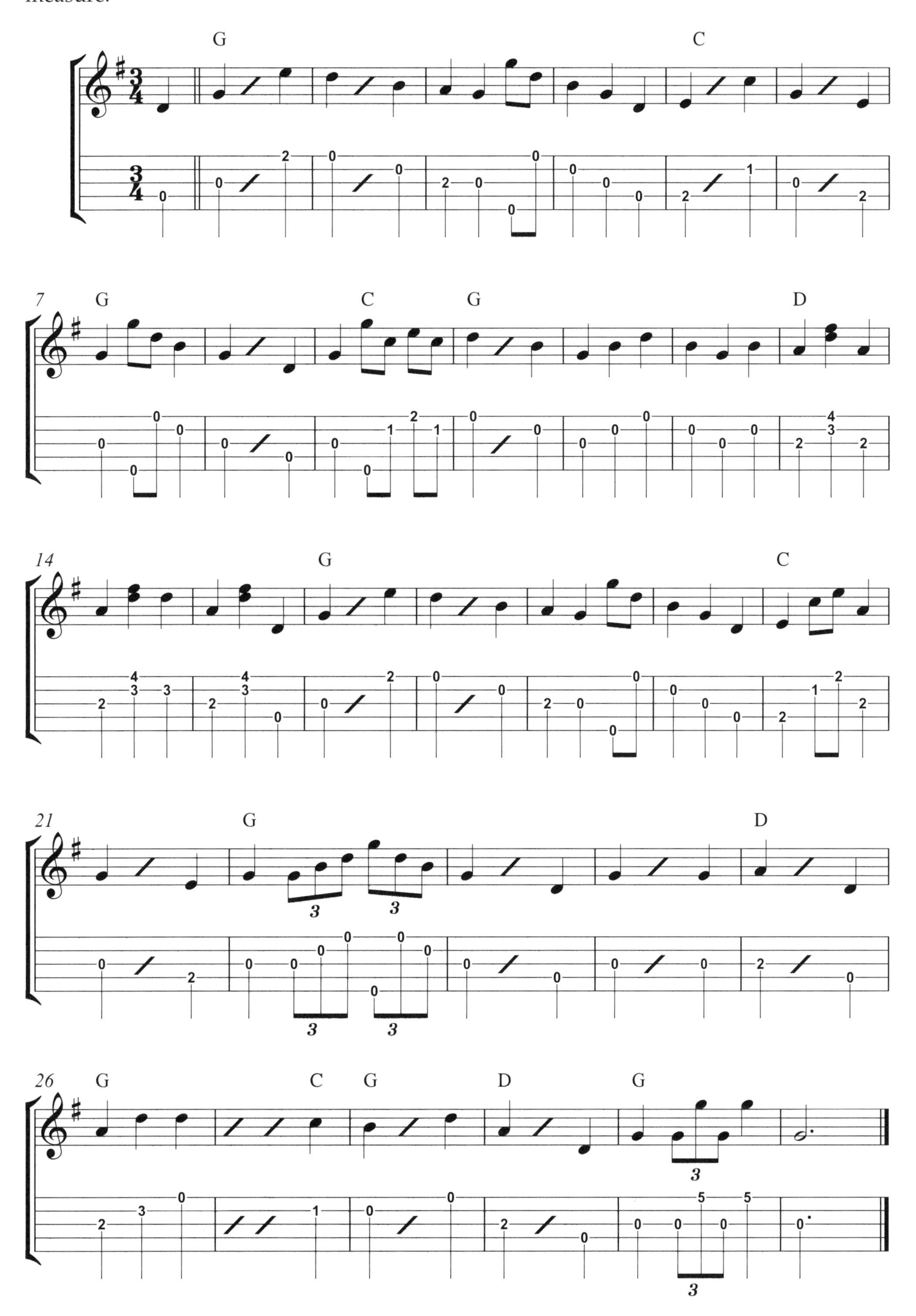

PART III: BUILDING A THUMB-LEAD STYLE BACKUP

I would now like to show how you can develop a thumb-lead backup for the song *A Dark Road is a Hard Road to Travel* as recorded by Grayson & Whitter on July 31, 1928 in New York City. First, here is the song:

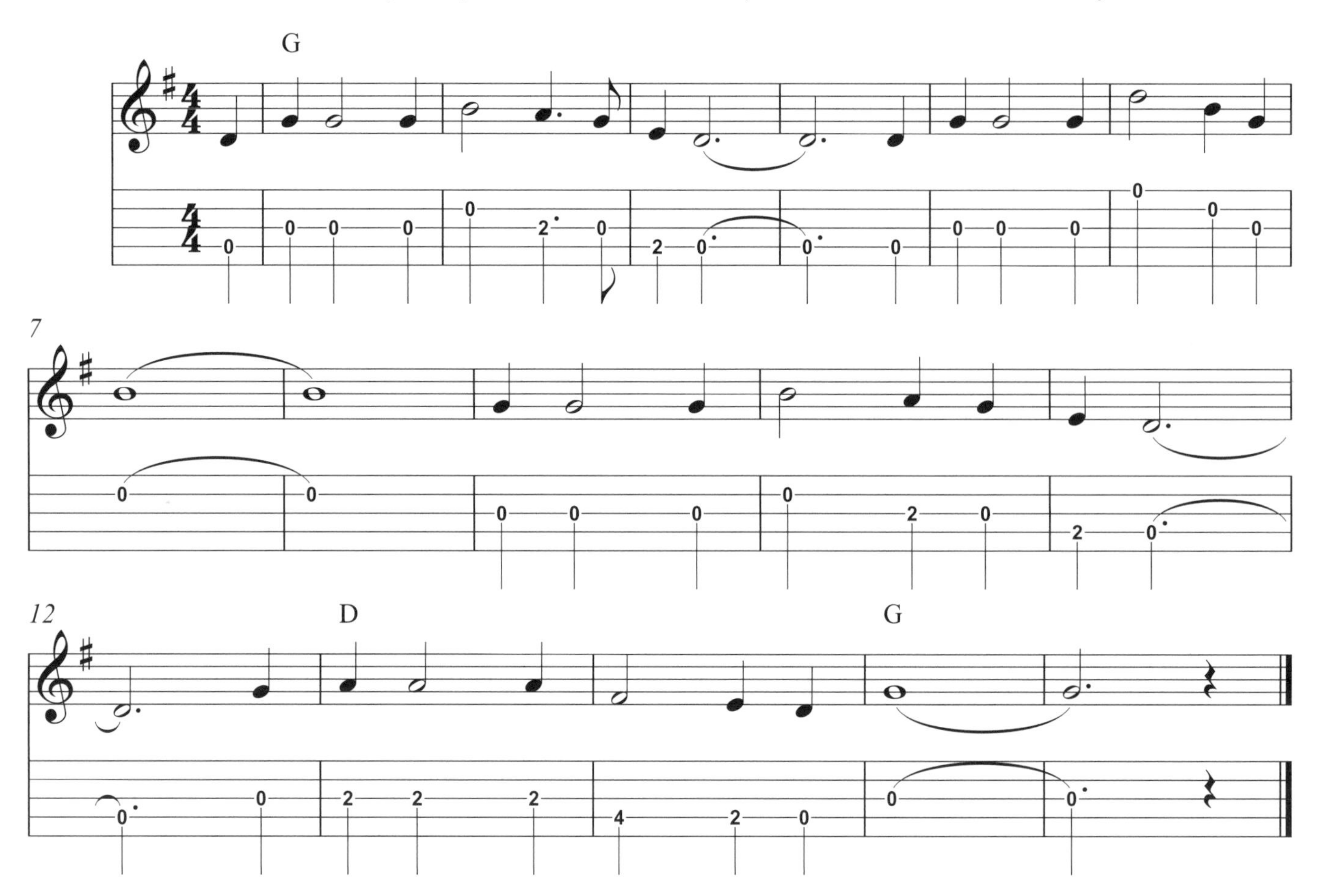

The song was recorded as follows:

Instrumental Introduction
Opening Verse
Instrumental Break

Verse
Verse
Instrumental Break

Verse
Verse
Instrumental Break

Closing Verse [same as first verse]

Closing Instrumental Break with short tag

For the opening instrumental break you could use the following backup that focuses on using the basic pinch pattern with the single note played only on the third string:

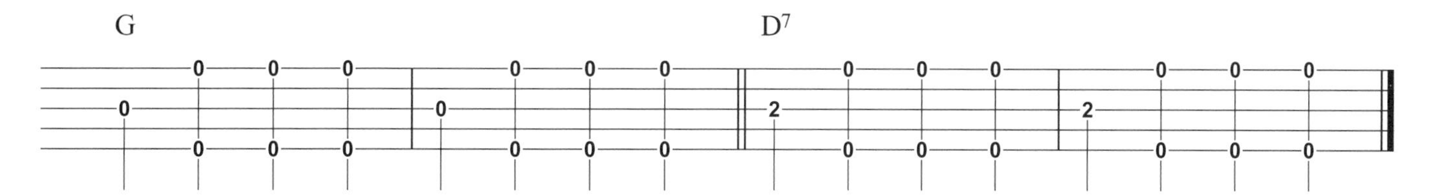

Next is a backup that you might use to play behind the verse:

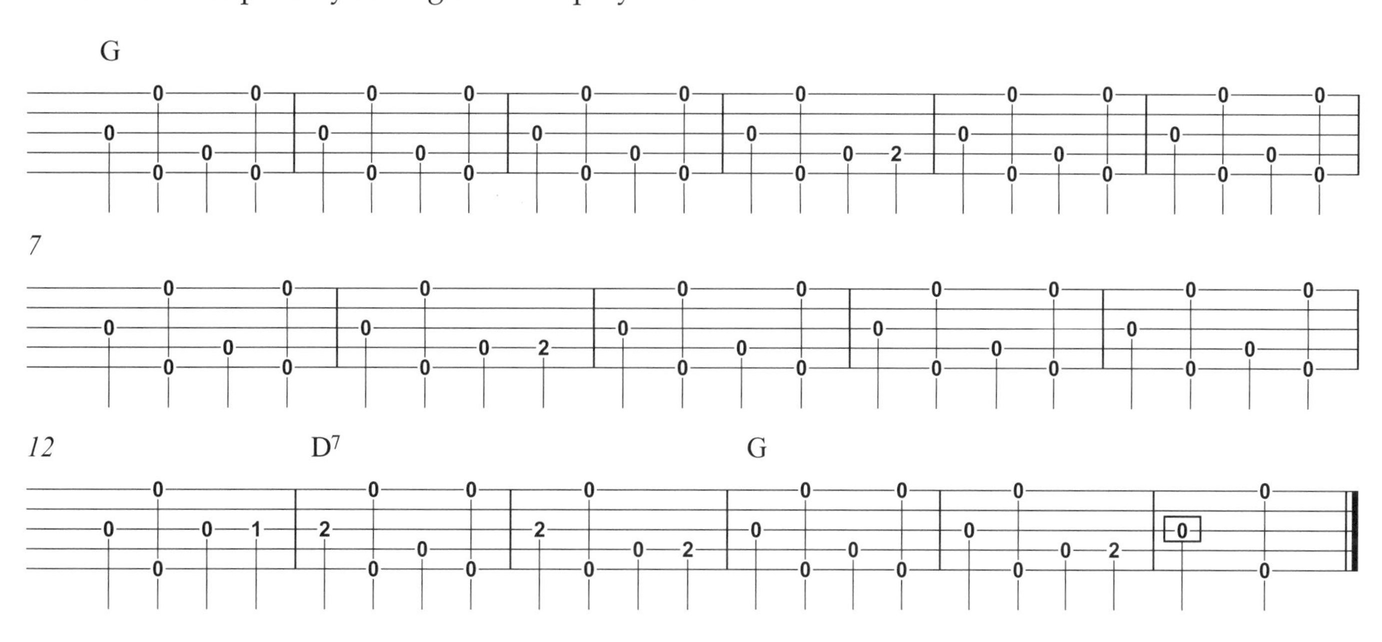

As you can see, this backup features an alternating bass note element.

Next is a different backup that you might use behind the instrumental breaks:

Next is a banjo solo of the melody:

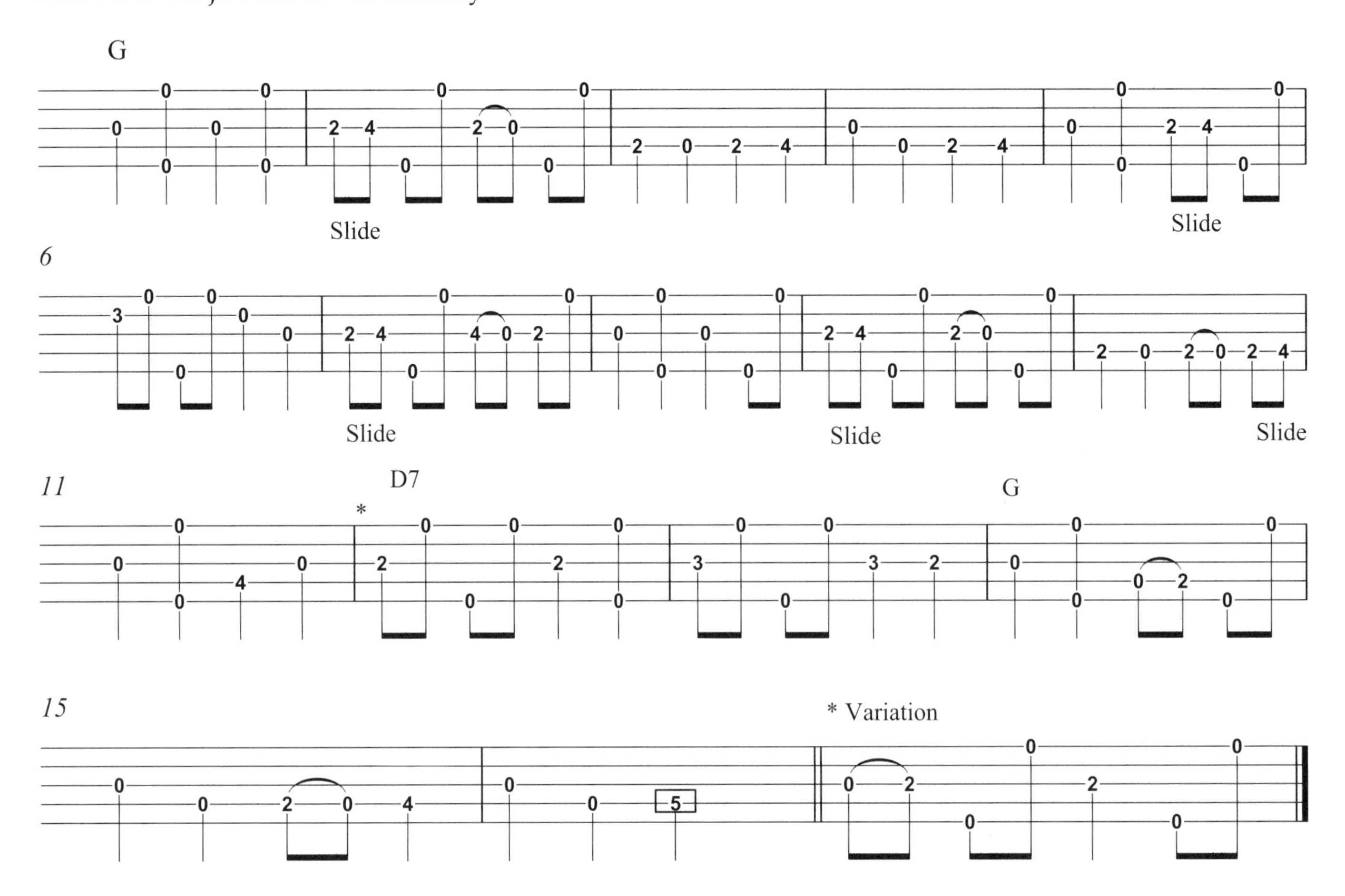

A final lick that you can incorporate is the Lunsford index finger brushing lick that I discussed earlier. Once again, here is the basic comparison:

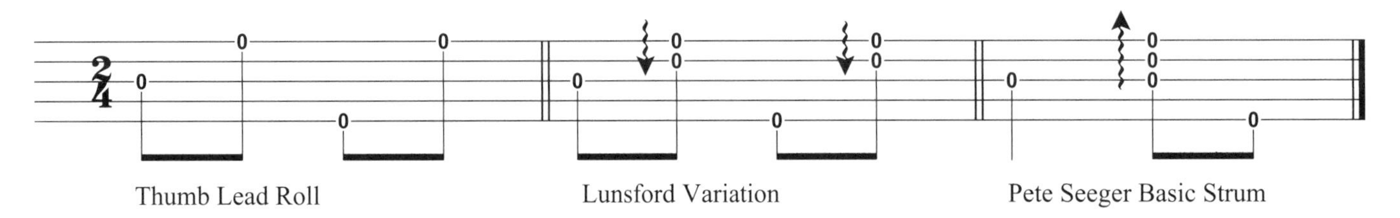

You could insert this roll at the conclusion of the verse before each of the instrumental breaks or over the short tag that concludes the song; you could also experiment using it over the entire closing instrumental "out chorus" break as well.

AFTERWORD

The arranging style for string band banjo backups during the 1920s was based on four performance styles -- banjo style (clawhammer), finger style, thumb lead and index lead -- although some extracurricular ones, such as the use of strummed chords or doubling the melody, were used. "Up the neck" note sequences were commonly featured in backups and solos; this should come as no surprise as songs and dances which appeared in banjo methods were routinely arranged using basic triad inversion chord shapes in a variety of fingerboard positions. However, while frequent use of the open fifth string was used in the lower positions it was rarely employed when playing "up the neck" because its function as a high-pitched drone was compromised, thus its use was reserved for the most part as a passing tone in scales, in chord outlines, or when shifting positions.

By 1933 the effects of the Depression was reflected in a dramatic decline in record sales; thus, some record companies were gradually forced to cancel recording contracts with their artists if, in fact, the company hadn't already gone bankrupt. As a result, the popular "old time music" artists of this Golden Age of recordings slipped into oblivion. The record industry began to rebound a few years later when musical tastes began to change, influenced by radio and movies: cowboys playing guitars (Gene Autry and Tex Ritter), the new western swing band format of Bob Wills or Sons of the Pioneers (with the then unknown Roy Rogers), national radio broadcasts of "barn dances" (Chicago's National Barn Dance on WLS and Nashville's Grand Ole Opry on WSM), and "brother acts" like Bill and Charlie Monroe, Anton and Rabon Delmore, Zeke and Wiley Morris, and the Blue Sky Boys (Bill and Earl Bolick).

Many of the techniques I have outlined in this book were commonly used by urban banjoists, in one form or another, during the "folk era" revival of the late 1950s/early 1960s, including the occasional use of syncopated bluegrass rolls or use of the syncopated West Indies 3-3-2 clave rhythm used in calypso-type songs that became popular during the 1950s (thanks to Harry Belafonte). The common source of 5-string folk banjo instruction available at that time was Pete Seeger's *How to play the 5-string Banjo* (originally printed by him in 1948, with a timely revised edition appearing in 1954), or at the local coffee house, college folk music club or hootenanny where you could trade licks with your peers in the honored folk tradition.

I would like to thank noted banjo historian Dr. Eli Kaufman, longtime editor of the American Banjo Fraternity's FIVE-STRINGER newsletter, along with his wife, Madeleine, for his critical comments on Part I that solidified certain historical facts.

I wish you the best exploring these banjo techniques and I hope that they provide you with a few ideas that you can incorporate in your banjo performances.

Joe Weidlich
Washington, DC
May 2013

APPENDICES

TRANSITIONAL SOLOS

As I mentioned in the Afterword, the basic techniques used by the southern string band banjoists were still in use for many years afterward into the folk era of the late 1950s and early 1960s. One reason for this is because the idiomatic techniques involved are straight forward vs. the intricacies of Scruggs style bluegrass banjo which involve the knowledge of eight or nine basic roll patterns, how to incorporate melodic notes within those rolls, the treatment of syncopation, and adjusting to the use of fingerpicks. Clawhammer banjo, in particular, enjoyed a renaissance around 1965 with the release of a series of albums by County Records of traditional clawhammer artists such as Wade Ward, Kyle Creed, Fred Cockerham and, later, Tommy Jarrell; and, in the 1970s, with the emergence of old time music revival bands like the Hollow Rock String Band, the Fuzzy Mountain String Band, and the Highwoods String Band.

Wade Mainer is frequently cited as one of the early pioneers in the formation of the 3-finger style of playing the banjo, particularly in his use of the thumb-lead style roll. However, here are two examples of his basic backup style during the post Depression years that he frequently used in recordings with his group, Wade Mainer's Mountaineers. The first example is based solely on guitar style techniques:

Regular C Tuning

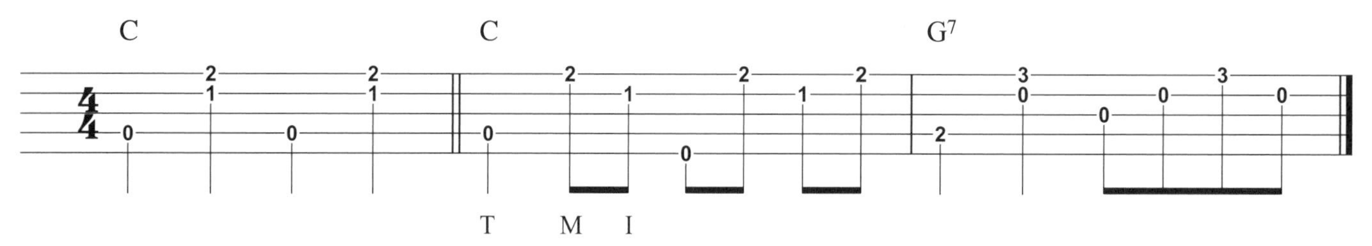

Having said that, we can see from the following 16-measure solo of the song *Come Back to Your Dobie Shack* that here it is based mostly on index lead (most of the backup is played out of the 7th position):

G Tuning

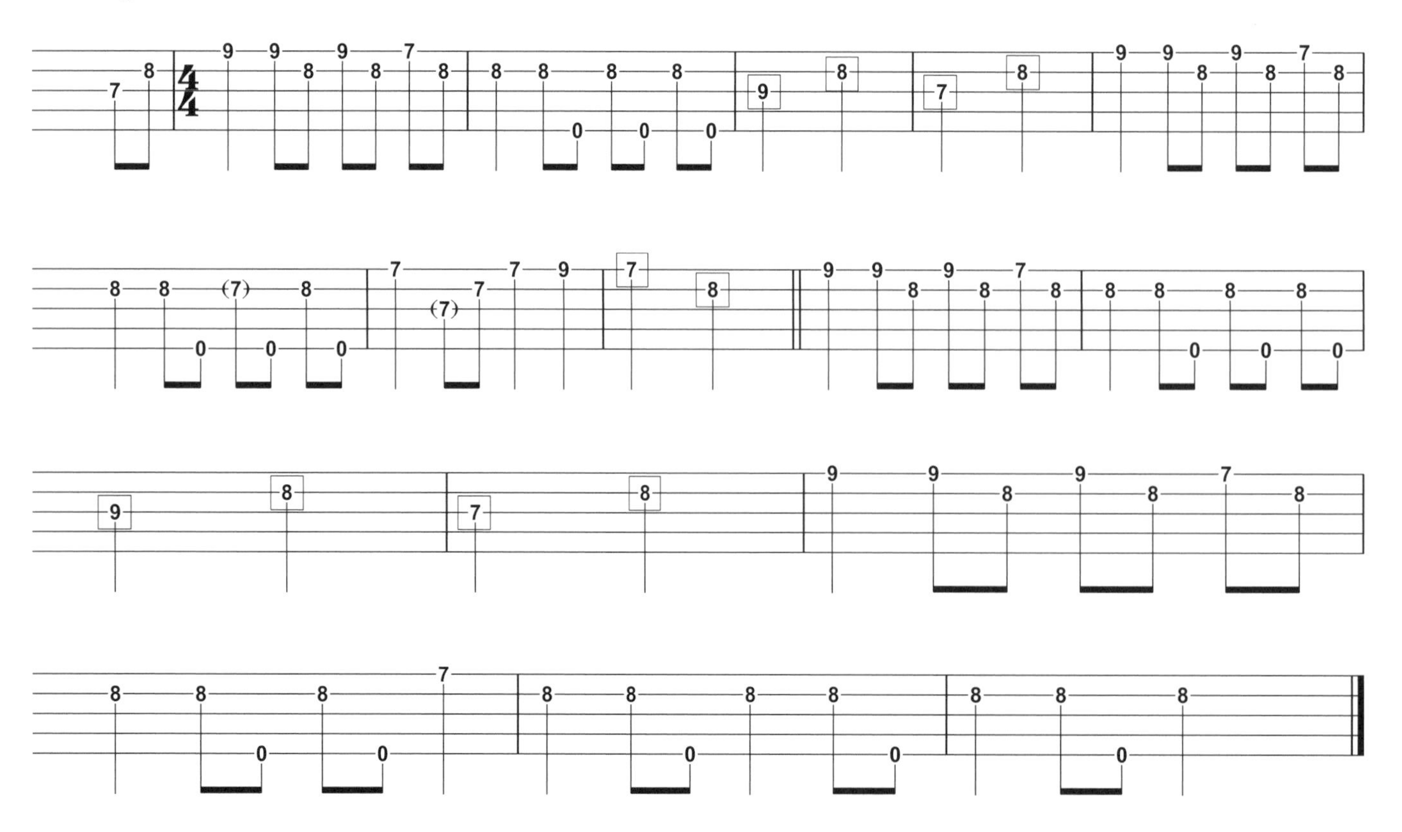

Let's move ahead a decade to compare Mainer's solo style with one played by **Dave "Stringbean" Akeman** on the song *True Life Blues*, as recorded by Bill Monroe and His Blue Grass Boys on February 13, 1945. The reason for this choice is that Akeman's solo consisted of elements based on both the index-lead and guitar styles, proving the point that the transformation of the use of these classic banjo patterns was awaiting the genius of Earl Scruggs to create and organize a logical style of playing the banjo in a syncopated fashion based on those styles, particularly thumb-lead (as Scruggs rarely used index-lead).

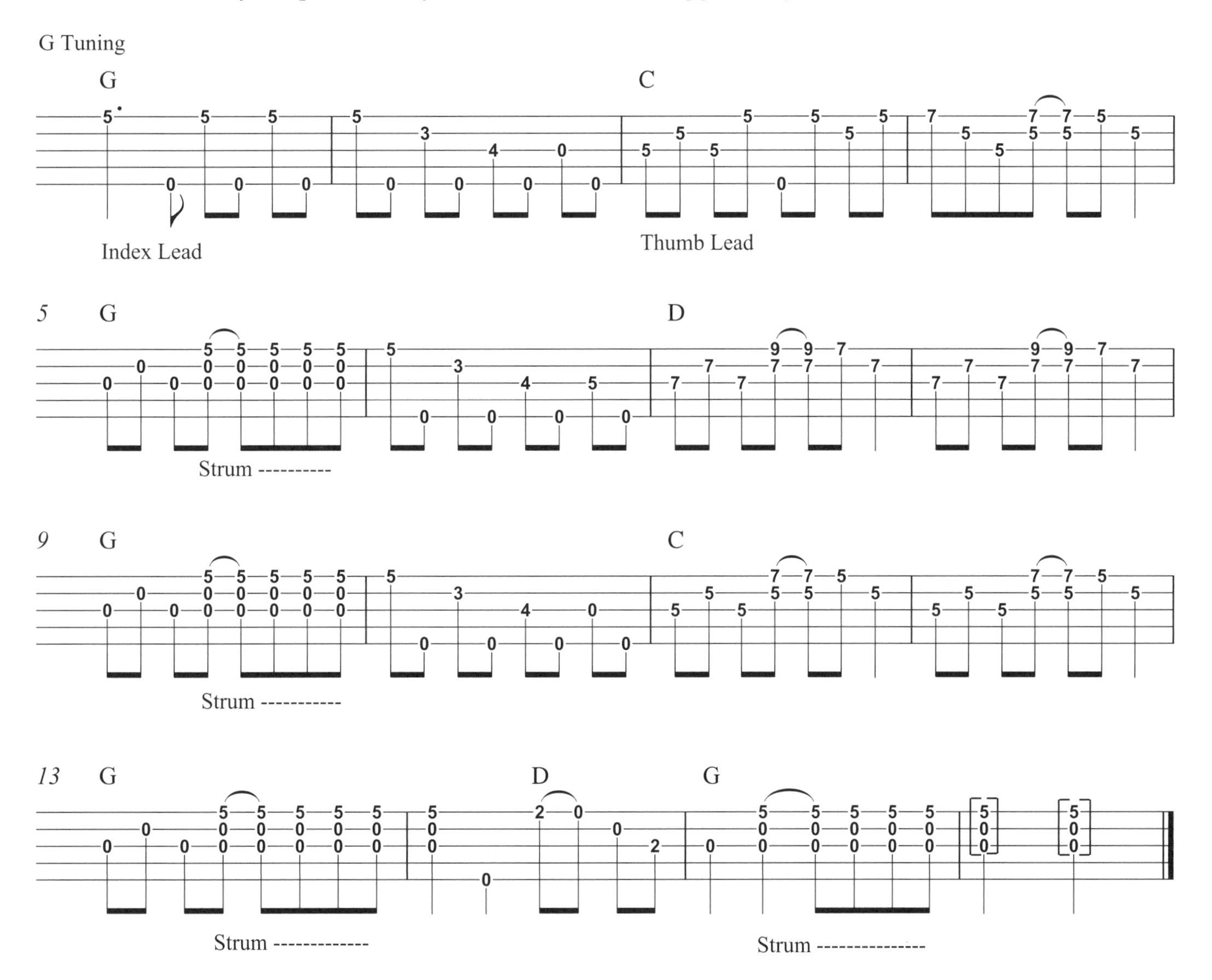

A few things to take particular note of here is the alternating thumb-roll pattern used in measure 3; the syncopated rhythmic figure in the following measure, as well in measures 7, 8, and 11; the strummed chords in measures 5, 9, 13 and 15; the use of a passing tone on beat four in measure 6; and the concluding tag roll used in measure 14. As Akeman missed his cue to begin his solo, I have to assume that as he was recovering what he played in measures 3 and 4 was not planned; what he actually played in measures 11 and 12 was probably what he intended to play in measures 3 and 4.

Another song recorded that day by the group was *Blue Grass Special.* Akeman's solo is similar in nature, so I advise that you listen to both and then compare the two.

Let's also include the solo to the song *Little Maggie*, as recorded by **Ralph Stanley** in late 1947-early 1948, a few months after the formation of the Stanley Brothers and the Clinch Mountain Boys (when this cut was recorded Stanley was not yet versed in Scruggs style banjo; later that year his first solo using Scruggs style picking would be on the new Bill Monroe song *Molly and Tenbrook*). Here, his solo is based on thumb-lead style, with some syncopated elements contained in measures 2, 3, 6 and 7:

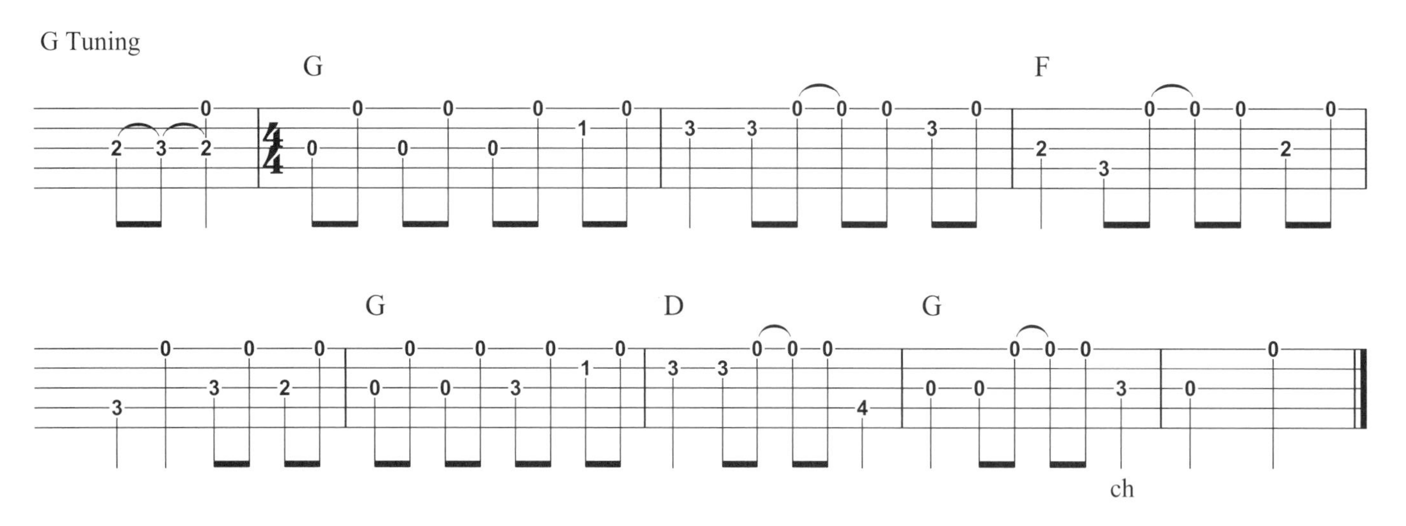

Dr. Humphrey Bate and his Possum Hunters

SELECTED BIBLIOGRAPHY

Bluegrass: A History by Neil V. Rosenberg
(University of Illinois Press, 1985)

Clawhammer Banjo by Miles Krassen (Oak Publications, 1974)

Country Music Originals: The Legends and the Lost by Tony Russell
(Oxford University Press, 2007)

Creating Country Music: Fabricating Authenticity by Richard A. Peterson
(The University of Chicago Press, 1997)

How to play the 5-string Banjo by Pete Seeger
(distributed by Music Sales Corporation)

Old-Time Mountain Banjo by Art Rosenbaum (Oak Publications, 1968)

Rambling Blues: The Life & Songs of Charlie Poole by Kinney Rorrer (1982)

By Joseph Weidlich:
George Knauff's *Virginia Reels* [arranged for guitar] (Centerstream Publications)

Minstrel Banjo—Brigg's Banjo Instructor (Centerstream Publications)

More Minstrel Banjo: Frank Converse's *Banjo Instructor, Without A Master*
(Centerstream Publications)

The Early Minstrel Banjo: Its Technique and Repertoire (Centerstream Publications)

AUTHOR'S BIOGRAPHY

Joseph Weidlich began his formal musical studies on the classic guitar, moving to Washington, D.C. from his native St. Louis to teach that instrument. He published a series of renaissance lute transcriptions for classic guitar which were distributed by G. Schirmer. In the early music genre he has played renaissance guitar, renaissance lute and baroque guitar.

Over the last 15 years Weidlich has written a number of books on 1920s-early 1930s string band music, early country guitar backup styles, Swing Era jazz guitar, and antebellum banjo styles. Reviews of his books have appeared in Acoustic Guitar magazine, the Old Time Herald, Banjo Newsletter, the Ozark Mountaineer and Dirty Linen. Weidlich has also written articles which have appeared in music journals and newsletters which have subsequently been cited as source material in related research and early music doctoral dissertations including *Battuto Performance Practice in Early Italian Guitar Music (1606-1637)* for the Journal of the Lute Society of America (Volume XI) which outlined the various strumming practices found in early guitar methods published in Italy and Spain in the early 17th century.